Universal Design Daily

365 Ways to Teach, Support, & Challenge All Learners

by

Dr. Paula Kluth

ISBN-13: 978-1537167466

Cover Illustration by Taryl Hansen

Additional Illustrations by Vecteezy.com & Shutterstock.com

Book Designed and Typeset by Kevin Fitzgerald

Printed in the United States of America

Contents

Preface

Are you ...

⟹ Tired of your same old assessments?

⟹ Seeking lesson formats that will challenge your students?

⟹ Looking for apps or websites to make learning more accessible?

⟹ In need of ideas that will help you collaborate more creatively?

⟹ Interested in "hacks" you can use to make planning for all more efficient and effective?

If you answered "yes" to any or all of these questions, you have chosen the right book to skim; read; re-read; highlight; mark up with pencils, markers, and sticky notes; and share with colleagues! This user-friendly guide will help you learn more about universal design by exploring the practices associated with it.

What Is UDL?

Universal Design for Learning (UDL) is a framework that inspires the development of learning environments and experiences that are flexible, responsive, and relevant for all students (Meyer, Rose & Gordon, 2014; Rose, 2001; Rose & Meyer, 2002). The model calls for creating curriculum, instruction, and assessment that provides

› multiple methods of engagement to tap into students' interests, challenge them appropriately, and motivate them to learn;

› multiple methods of action and expression to provide alternatives for demonstrating learning and understanding; and

› multiple methods of representation to give learners various ways of acquiring information and knowledge.

In a nutshell, UDL is intended to boost student motivation and achievement by reducing physical, cognitive, and organizational barriers to learning.

UDL is a powerful model for lesson design because it asks educators to consider student needs, abilities, interests, and learning goals before they begin to plan. This is in stark contrast to the approach that teachers might have taken in the past where the lessons are planned and then adapted or changed post-design to meet the needs of one or more students with unique learning profiles.

In universally-designed lessons, teachers consider how to teach all students from the get-go. They may present content using more than one mode of output. They may invite students to show what they know via skits, demonstrations, three-page papers, teacher-led interviews, or Animoto (www.animoto.com) presentations. They may allow students to read and learn about a novel using a range of tools and supports including potentially, a book, an audio book, an e-reader, a video clip of key scenes, and a visual thesaurus like Visuwords (www.visuwords.com). It is important to understand that these options are not intended to support some students, they are an attempt to make both information and learning accessible, relevant, and engaging for all.

Some descriptions of UDL—even those just provided—may cause some educators to feel a bit overwhelmed. You may be thinking, "Do I need to use five different methods of assessment in every lesson?" or "How many tools must I provide for composition?" The answer is simple. You need to provide what your students need to be successful. So if a choice of two assessment tools gives all students an opportunity to successfully demonstrate learning, then you need just two assessment tools. In addition, keep in mind that developing a lesson for UDL doesn't always require the latest app, device, or tech tool. Universal design may include those things, certainly, but—as you will see in this book—music; writing, sketching, and journaling; video clips and movies; cooperative learning games; drama activities; collaborative structures; visual supports and pictures; toys and props; models; and art are also part of the UDL classroom. The intention of this model is to interest, support, and appropriately challenge every single learner, every single day.

Why "Universal Design Daily"?

For the last 25 years, I have been teaching teachers and otherwise supporting them in my work as a consultant, writer, and education researcher. In this work, I am always looking for ways to help busy educators learn strategies and implement supports to use in their increasingly diverse classrooms. The teachers I meet are eager to try new approaches to meet the needs of their students, but they are short on time.

As a former elementary and high school teacher, I know it can feel overwhelming to keep up with new models, methods, and materials. This book is designed to support any educator who does not have time to search websites for hours, attend a series of workshops, or read a multi-chapter book cover-to-cover in order to plan effective and appropriately-challenging lessons.

The book has 365 ideas so that readers can focus on just one idea per day, but if you are an overachiever, feel free to flip through at your own pace. Read two a day if you dare or even all 365 in one sitting!

I have divided the content of this book into three sections to make browsing as easy as possible:

Section I: Understanding UDL

This introduction to the book consists of two categories. The ABCs of UDL is designed to help you prepare to use UDL in your classroom, and PD for UDL provides ideas for UDL-related professional development.

The first ideas presented in this book are there to acquaint you with the UDL model. These 29 suggestions provide guidance on classroom management, learning about students, and preparing learning spaces. This part of the book isn't so much about the students as it is about the teacher; it will help you get ready to work in the UDL classroom.

The second category in this section, PD for UDL, is similar to the first in that it is teacher-focused. It is different in that it is completely centered on professional development and adult learning. These ideas provide guidance on forming a Profession-

al Learning Community (PLC), locating appropriate resources, collaborating with colleagues, and more.

Section II: Teaching & Learning with UDL

Here you can explore ideas related to the three principles of UDL. You will find dozens of ideas for providing multiple methods of engagement, multiple methods of action and expression, and multiple methods of representation.

In the multiple methods of engagement pages, you will find ideas for supporting student self-regulation, optimizing motivation, encouraging reflection, clarifying and communicating goals, and allowing choice-making. *Day 77: Book It*, for instance, provides guidance on creating book clubs in the UDL classroom; this strategy provides choices about reading materials, allows students to work in teams, and encourages them to manage their own learning and support the learning of others.

Following the dozens of engagement ideas, you will find recommendations for offering different methods of action and expression. You will learn techniques for guiding goal setting, supporting strategy development, using multiple tools for construction and composition, varying methods for response, optimizing access to technologies, and more. For instance, on *Day 132: Be Comical*, options for using comic strips in the classroom are outlined. Purposes for using comics are shared and several different comic-creating tools are recommended.

In the final pages of this section, you will find suggestions for providing multiple methods of representation in the classroom. You will find ideas for activating background knowledge, highlighting big ideas and essential questions, learning new vocabulary and symbols, and providing options for perception. *Day 186: Level It Out*, for instance, highlights how to teach a novel or play using a variety of texts, images, and tech tools. The suggestions provided help students with different needs and abilities access the same content.

Section III: Using UDL & Beyond

This part of the book features strategies that don't fit neatly into any one area of the UDL model. I have added tips and ideas related to ideology and beliefs, collaboration, technology, learning environment, teaching strategies, and lesson design. Some suggestions may not relate directly to any UDL principle, but will otherwise help you support students in your diverse, inclusive classroom. Other ideas work well in two or all three areas of the UDL model; they might help you provide multiple methods of engagement and multiple methods of representation, for example. *Day 299: Use That Tune* is one such idea. It encourages the use of music to teach and inspire. This recommendation certainly is an example of engagement, as music can be very motivating for a wide range of learners. Using music as a transition, however, would also be an example of representation as it is an alternative to visual cues and supports.

When Do I Start?

So, now that you have just a little background on the book's purpose, content, and design, you are ready to read. Go for it!

I hope *Universal Design Daily* will be just the boost you need to try something new or to keep implementing a technique you already use. Whatever your purpose for reading, I am confident that this little book will be a handy companion as you commit to creating universally-designed lessons every single day.

Section I

Understanding UDL

ABC

ABCs of UDL

Day **1**

Get The Room Ready

While a great teacher can undoubtedly support the needs of all learners in a less-than-organized classroom, it makes the work so much easier when spaces and materials are in order. To get organized in your UDL classroom, try the following ideas:

> Divide up the space. Break your classroom into different learning areas, if possible. For example, you might create a small storage area, a classroom library corner, and a project center. This allows you to easily direct different types of work groups into the most appropriate spaces (e.g., "If you are partner reading, move to the library") and sort materials in ways that make the most sense for daily use.

> Review resources. If you have a bin that houses unclaimed papers, be sure that students know where it is and when they can peruse it. If you have learning games that students can check out, be sure everyone knows where they are stored and any guidelines for borrowing them.

> Label materials. This will help students participate as independently as possible in daily lessons, rituals, and routines and make it easier for them to both set up and clean up activities.

> Create a command center. Set up a space where students can check the weekly calendar; find extra paper, pencils, and chargers; and submit hard copies of assigned work.

Day 2

Add One At A Time

Gradually add new pieces to your UDL model. You might start with implementing a wider range of assessments and then design a few tiered lessons. Once you feel comfortable with these practices, try some whole-class response techniques or plan some lessons with a new collaborative partner. Continue to add to your model as you discover new approaches, tools, and strategies.

Play Favorites

Some teachers in diverse classrooms worry that they spend too much time focused on their students with unique learning profiles, and not enough time focused on those with needs that are not as obvious. On certain days, or during some lessons, this may be the case. In any classroom, some students will simply require more teacher support, feedback, and attention than others.

Teachers in these classrooms may need help to focus on the individual needs of all their students. To reach that goal, create a pile of index cards (one for each student in your class) and flip over a new one each day to pick a new "favorite." This individual gets special treatment. You can set aside a few extra minutes to socialize with this learner, take more time to examine his or her written work, or call home to share some good news with that student's family.

Secondary teachers might create a less-structured version of this game by picking a letter of the day and "playing favorites" with some or all of the students whose names begin with that letter.

Day 4

Ask Your Administrator

Don't go it alone. Ask your administrators for assistance in pursuing your UDL-related goals. Look for conferences on related topics (e.g., blended learning, problem-based learning, brain-based teaching) and ask for support to attend, or suggest inviting speakers on these topics to your district or school. Ask to be observed by any district or building administrators who have expertise on the topic, or seek permission to observe lessons in other UDL-focused district classrooms. Finally, consider talking to your administrator about accessing UDL-related resources, such as planning time with colleagues, new assistive technology tools, or accessible classroom furnishings (e.g., standing desks).

Day 5

Ask For One

A critical aspect of designing lessons for all is getting feedback. How can you get this feedback quickly, regularly, and honestly? Ask your students!

Give each one of your students a single index card and ask them to record one thing you could do to encourage their success and support their engagement. In order to get the best possible responses, you may need to provide them with a few examples, or give them time to discuss the prompt with a partner before responding.

Collect and read the cards.

Then, do your best to integrate some of the suggestions immediately so that your students understand that their voices are valued. Revisit the feedback regularly to get ideas for responding to the learning differences in your classroom.

Repeat the exercise any time you need a little inspiration.

Day 6
Consult The Consumer

Make students your partners in creating a classroom that works well for everyone. Don't do UDL to them, do it with them.

Explain your thinking about lesson design. Enlist their help in making sure the classroom runs smoothly. Get their input on which instructional approaches work best for them. For some skills or concepts, ask your learners, "How do you think you could learn this best?" Provide concrete choices (e.g., creating a model, designing a lab), but be open to their ideas, too.

Keep in mind that consulting with your "consumers" is not only a strategy for making the classroom more democratic, but a clever way to get students engaged in the curriculum before it is even taught.

Day 7

Design for All Daily

Vary the learning experiences in your classroom regularly. Lecture and whole-class discussions will likely be part of your day even if you teach small children, but learners should see dozens of approaches to teaching and learning every month in their classrooms.

Do you regularly incorporate learning games, small-group work, demonstrations, collaborative structures, peer teaching and tutoring, learning stations, and project-based instruction in your classroom? How about tech tools, video, music, and drama? How varied are your assessments? Keep asking these questions and keep growing your model.

Day 8

Teach, Practice, Repeat

When you introduce a new learning strategy (especially one that you want students to engage in independently), coach them until they have mastered it. Then add another. For example, if you want to teach partner reading or peer editing, be sure to take time to teach the skills related to those practices; observe and provide feedback as the skills are used; and repeat the process until mastery is achieved. Teaching strategies once won't likely have much of an impact but, if you take some time to provide guidance in this area on an ongoing basis, you will eventually have a group of learners who know your expectations, have the skills to work independently, and make it possible for you to provide a range of UDL-related supports in the classroom (e.g., conferencing with individual students or small groups).

Day 9

Wait

In some classrooms, teachers may assume that—due to their diverse population of learners—some students will always need something a little different to effectively participate in daily lessons (e.g., a peer partner, a piece of assistive technology). With the increased focus on designing lessons in a more universal and accessible way, however, this assumption may not be accurate.

For each lesson you create, assess whether or not certain supports or changes are necessary. Will some students need additional materials, or are there already enough available to support learning? Do you need to create unique roles for some learners or does the lesson already allow them to learn in different ways and make varied contributions? Is more personal support necessary for certain students, or is collaboration already built into the lesson? Add extra support if necessary, of course, but assess before you do.

 **Day 10**

Make The Most Of The Minutes

Engage students in purposeful tasks from the minute they walk into the classroom.

To make this recommendation easy to implement, create a routine. For instance, if you are a math teacher, have a challenge problem or mental math exercise prepared for students as they enter the room. If you teach language arts, you might require 10 minutes of journal writing as the first task on the agenda each day.

The activities do not necessarily need to be academic in nature, they just need to be purposeful. For example, a fourth-grade teacher who asks students to come in each day and begin guided meditations on their iPads is making the most of classroom minutes by preparing students to learn. This task not only gets students focused the minute they walk in the door, but it also serves as a centering transition ritual that can support learners both emotionally and academically.

Day 11

Ask To Be Assessed

Most educators would agree that they profit from student feedback on their teaching. Unfortunately, these same teachers may not have a formal way to collect this feedback. One quick and easy way to do so is to develop a report card, and allow learners to evaluate you, your daily lessons, and the learning environment. Aside from learning about the needs of individual students, you may also uncover trends that will inform your teaching. For instance, do boys and girls rate classroom activities the same or differently? Do first-period learners ask for more movement than third-period learners? Do morning students see you as a more enthusiastic teacher than your afternoon students?

Day 12

Get Started On Day One

Don't use the first few days of school to cover rules and policies alone. Dive in to rich content immediately and link activities to community building so you can achieve a bit more. For instance, you can introduce great poets and poems by having students peruse a few samples and share their favorites with the class. This can be a powerful getting-to-know-you exercise, as learners can introduce themselves by sharing their selection, explaining their choice, and talking about what it means to them. Likewise, if you want to teach about collaborative behaviors and norms on the first day, you could have students solve a complex math problem in small groups. As they address content-area material, you can provide feedback on their listening and problem-solving skills.

Smile For The Camera

Don't keep your great ideas to yourself! Set up a wiki or YouTube channel and ask your colleagues to contribute short video clips (3–5 minutes) of differentiation or UDL techniques they have successfully implemented in their classrooms. These clips can feature either an explanation of a strategy or a segment of an actual lesson.

This practice will help every educator in the building expand the range of strategies they use, and learn about the areas of expertise of their colleagues. Videos can help everyone in the building identify who they can turn to for advice in strengthening their UDL know-how in any number of subject or skill areas. Furthermore, creating videos can be inspiration to try something new; often, the very act of creating a product for others to view serves as an inspiration to impress and, perhaps, think a little outside the box.

Stock Up

Head to the warehouse store, garage sale, or teacher supply shop. You need to get your room ready for your universally-designed lessons. Some of the supplies you may want to have on hand include

> - rolling carts that you can use for portable learning centers (especially useful in secondary classrooms where tables might be in short supply);
>
> - colored cardstock, paper, and index cards to use for differentiating directions/tasks/assignments;
>
> - a large bin of clipboards so that students can work anywhere including on the floor;
>
> - portable timers to keep small groups on track;

> - mailboxes (e.g., magazine holders, stacked boxes) to house personalized reading recommendations, notes, and enrichment materials;
>
> - large dry-erase boards to record step-by-step directions for group work or different stations; and
>
> - bulletin board or poster board to list enrichment/extension ideas.

Day 15

Keep It Up

In the last few weeks of school, there is still so much learning that can and should take place. Use these last days of the year to implement some of the UDL techniques you have been meaning to try. Think about what you have taught during the year and what might need to be reviewed or re-taught.

Even if you have a lot of busy work to do in these last days, keep the learning going. Play an educational podcast for students to listen to as they clean out their desks. As you discuss final assessments with students one-on-one, keep other students busy researching an area of interest, or exploring new content-rich websites.

Don't quit until the bell rings on the last day.

Connect

In as many lessons as possible, try to speak with every student in your classroom. For some lessons, this will be easy. For instance, if students are working in five small groups and you can coach each of the groups in one hour, you will have connected with every learner. If students are working individually or in pairs, however, this may be trickier. In this instance, you may not get all the way around the room. Instead, you can connect with a handful of students and check their names off on a list. During the next lesson, you can pick up where you left off and continue making connections and checking off names until you reach every learner. This practice—even if followed more informally—will help you assess student learning and provide extra challenge or support to those who need it.

Get Ready For Your Close Up

Decide what you want students to know and be able to do by the end of the school year. Then, create a series of short videos to teach some of these concepts and ideas. These clips can be posted online to allow students to view them multiple times, if needed.

The hardest part of this recommendation is getting started. Don't overthink it. Just turn on the camera and start teaching. Then view your work and consider how to "punch it up" a bit. Could you add a visual or two? Use a catch phrase? Integrate some props? Don a costume? Sing a song? Involve students in some way?

Your clips don't need every bell and every whistle, but they should be interesting or memorable enough to sustain students' attention and help them remember the targeted content.

Need help generating ideas for your videos? Review clips on Kahn Academy (www.khanacademy.org) and LearnZillion (www.learnzillion.com).

Pay Up

Make lesson design a breeze by collecting resources from other teachers. Just click on Teachers Pay Teachers (www.teacherspay-teachers.com) and begin to browse. Many of the items are free and others are available for just a few dollars. You are bound to find many supports for your UDL classroom here, including tic-tac-toe choice boards, learning games, flashcards, center activities, visuals, interactive notebook supplies, and review packets.

To get started search "UDL" or "differentiated instruction" and continue with more specific words and phrases to find materials related to your content area, grade level, and upcoming lessons.

See UDL As Dynamic

No two students or groups are the same; therefore, if you tier a lesson or offer three different assessment options one period, be aware that this may not be necessary for every group you teach that day. Further, this change in needs can happen not only from group to group, but also from week to week. The way you support, engage, and challenge students in September, will likely be different from how you support, engage, and challenge them in April or even in October. As your students' needs change and evolve, so should your lesson design practices.

Just Start

Feeling intimidated by the whole idea of universal design? Start slow. Choose one or two easy-to-tackle strategies to begin your quest for a more personalized classroom. Some of the easiest ways to respond to differences are

> asking open-ended questions or varied questions;

> providing a range of learning materials;

> introducing new technology tools (e.g., speech-recognition software, e-books, classroom response systems);

> implementing peer tutoring or cross-age tutoring;

> co-teaching a lesson or two with a neighboring teacher, related-services provider, or paraprofessional;

> varying student groupings (e.g., pairs, trios, small groups);

> using a wide range of assessment tools and strategies;

> giving choices (e.g., how to show understanding, which materials to use); and

> using cooperative learning structures.

Give A Makeover

Select a unit of study that you have taught in the past. Analyze it. Give it a makeover.

Ask yourself:

> Is it rigorous enough?

> Is it accessible for all?

> Is it interesting?

> Are the activities varied?

> Are there several ways for students to learn?

> Are there several ways for students to show what they know?

Once you answer these questions, decide how you might improve the unit plan. Pick just one or two things to address in your makeover. For instance, you might add a hook, change one of your assessments, or use new presentation software.

Narrow The Focus

Invite each teacher in your grade level team or department to study a specific area of UDL for a period of time, and ask that they be responsible for offering suggestions for that area. As you sit down to plan, one of you may focus on materials, another on technology, another on assessment, and still another on teaching strategies. Or you might break into three groups; one that studies multiple means of representation, one that looks into multiple means of action and expression, and one that focuses primarily on multiple means of engagement.

Be sure to follow up on the suggestions offered by having everyone reflect on what they tried, how it worked, and how it might be improved.

Put Procedures In Place

At the beginning of the school year, teach students procedures for

> entering the classroom,

> submitting daily work,

> turning in homework,

> getting books from the class library,

> using unstructured time,

> working with peers,

> using the restroom/leaving the room,

> getting into small groups,

> caring for tablets and computers, and

> storing and accessing materials.

Giving students this information empowers them to manage materials, time, and space. It also teaches them organization and self-management skills. Further, a "well-oiled" classroom shows respect for students and allows everyone to work effectively and efficiently.

Day 24

Create A Coffee Klatch

Different parents will want to make contributions to your school or classroom in different ways. Some like to tutor. Some want to co-ordinate the book fair. And some might want to put their creativity and teaching skills to work by creating supports for classrooms. If you need help designing lessons and creating related materials for students, enlist the help of your families. Assemble a group to create visual supports, classroom games, task cards, physical models, and other learning tools.

Provide a space for this group to work, treat them to some coffee and snacks, and provide clear guidelines for creating the materials you need.

You might host your UDL "coffee klatch" weekly or a few times per month. This group serves at least two purposes, the most obvious being to help teachers provide the best learning experiences possible. The second purpose is bringing together school community members to think about the diverse needs of students in the school.

Teach Alternatives To The Teacher

Teach students strategies for getting support when you're busy with another task (e.g., meeting with small groups). Some of the many strategies you can try include the following:

> Direct them to ask peers for help. Some teachers have rules about this and remind students to "ask three before me."

> Encourage them to rethink the need for help. Remind them to review their notes one more time or observe the work of others before asking for direction.

> Assign a student facilitator or classroom expert for certain lessons. This person may need to wear a lanyard or pin so they can be easily identified.

> Let students know about who can provide support, besides the teacher. For instance, if you have a paraprofessional in your classroom for certain parts of the day, he or she may be a resource.

> Create a visual (e.g., a brightly-colored index card) students can place on their desktops to indicate that they need help from a teacher or peer.

Break Barriers

Universal design is about more than just teaching and reaching all learners. It is also about breaking down barriers in the classroom and in daily lessons. Just as a street corner may be insurmountable to some wheelchair users without a curb cut, a lesson or room design flaw may make learning challenging or even impossible for one, a few, or all students in a class. Therefore, "curb cuts" must be put into place whenever a learning barrier is perceived.

To create a powerful UDL classroom, evaluate your learning spaces and activities and look for potential challenges or obstacles for students. Then, explore ways to eliminate them. For instance:

> If the preferred learning modality of most of the class is visual and the directions are primarily given verbally, this is a barrier. The barrier breaker is providing directions verbally and visually, whenever possible.

> If some students struggle mightily to write longhand, taking essay tests can be a barrier. The barrier breaker is allowing students a choice of writing tools for this task including computers, tablets, or speech-recognition software. Another barrier breaker would be allowing students to occasionally choose other assessments.

> If several students are uncomfortable because they are required to sit at their seats with their feet on the floor all day long, the seating arrangement and the rigid rule are both barriers. The barrier breaker is giving students seating choices throughout the day (e.g., sitting on the floor, using an exercise ball).

Prep & Plan

Some tools and materials needed by students with unique learning profiles are readily available in the classroom. Others can be slapped together on the fly. Still others, however, need to be designed and assembled in advance. Use these tips and tricks to get the work done:

› Ask for what you need. Looking for a 3-D model of the human eye? A neon yardstick? A large-print version of *Stuart Little*? You never know! There may be teachers in the building who have exactly what you are seeking.

› Look on Pinterest (www.pinterest.com) for inspiration. You will find downloadable materials, "hacks," and shortcuts for developing learning tools.

› Involve all team members in the creation of learning materials. Speech pathologists may want to help in the creation of low-tech tools that foster interaction and collaboration between students. Occupational therapists may want to contribute games and activities that promote movement. Literacy specialists may be happy to help teams expand the materials used in reading and writing instruction.

› Plan in advance for any down time. Paraprofessionals may have segments of time in their day or week when they do not need to provide direct support. This may happen when all students are busy in a large-group activity, when they go to a whole-school event, or even when one or more learners are absent. Be ready for these moments. Assemble a bin of raw materials (e.g., contact paper, construction paper, duct tape) and directions for creating the learning tools you want but have not yet been able to create. Plan well and you will have that magnetic bone cell, those world explorer task cards, and that adapted version of Chapter 9 in the Spanish textbook, sooner rather than later.

Just Tweak It

Many teachers are wary of UDL because they believe it involves creating several different learning experiences within each lesson, or that choices, varied materials, and active learning options need to be offered constantly. All of those pieces are part of universal design, but every strategy need not be part of every lesson or even every day.

The truth is, some of the best UDL strategies involve a simple tweak or small change in plans to ensure that certain students will find the lesson more accessible, relevant, or appropriately challenging. For example:

> Some students may struggle with writing and, therefore, need to use a tablet or computer to take weekly quizzes.

> Several learners may produce higher-quality work if they can brainstorm with peers before producing written responses on their exit tickets.

> During a literacy centers lesson, it might be best for one or two students to skip some centers and repeat others in order to provide them with additional skill practice in key areas of need.

> One student may need to use adapted equipment (e.g., rocking knife, weighted cutlery) to prepare and eat a meal in a foods class.

> Everyone in the class may be more motivated to complete the math review if they are allowed to choose how they want to study (e.g., using a game on a website, working with a partner, or completing problems in the textbook).

Sponge Up The Excess

Throughout the day, there may be times when students finish work early. In these moments, it is helpful for them to know what they can do until the next activity or lesson is introduced. Every teacher should designate tasks to "sponge up" the minutes at the end of the day, or when assigned work is completed. These tasks can also be used when students come in early from lunch or from an assembly.

In a UDL classroom, it is best to have a variety of activities for students to review and select. You can list these options on a poster, put them on a class wiki, or write options on craft sticks and let students draw them out of a cup when they need inspiration.

Options you can offer include

> working on a passion project or exploring a question of personal interest,

> reading a book or an online newspaper,

> creating a post for the classroom blog,

> watching one of the content-related videos earmarked for an upcoming unit,

> reviewing and revising learning portfolios, and

> helping a classmate with work (as appropriate).

PD for UDL

Day 30

Be Professional

If you are a teacher who learns best in and with a group, you may want to seek out a Professional Learning Community (PLC) to support your work in your UDL classroom. A PLC provides a structure for collaboration with colleagues, along with professional growth and development. These groups are formed for the specific purpose of improving classroom practices and achieving better results for students.

In some schools and districts, time to meet with a learning community is embedded into the school day. Through PLCs, teachers learn from each other, share best practices, analyze student data, and plan for instruction. In other words, PLCs typically focus on issues directly related to differentiation and Universal Design for Learning.

If your district is not formally promoting PLCs and you can't find other educators interested in forming one, you may want to find an online community. Online PLCs allow teachers to guide their own learning and collaboration. Wikispaces (**www.wikispaces.com**), Twitter (**twitter.com**), and Ning (**www.ning.com**) are all popular tools that can be used to support your group. Use them to chat with colleagues, post ideas, share goals, and report progress.

Day 31

Find A Coach

Is there is a teacher you admire for her implementation of new presentation tools, collaboration with the occupational therapist, or re-markable ability to collect and analyze data in the classroom? If so, ask her to throw a cap on her head and a whistle around her neck and serve—if only temporarily—as your UDL coach. Even if the colleague you choose does not have time to offer a lot of support, he or she may be willing to look at your plans, introduce you to a new technique, or even co-teach a few lessons with you.

Write To Learn

Blog, write a newsletter article, or compose a longer article for publication. No matter what you do or how you do it, you will find that writing about your practice will move you forward in your work. Most teachers choose writing topics related to areas of great success in their work, but if you are struggling in one particular area of your practice, you might want to write about how you are overcoming challenges and working to learn new skills.

Teachers often crave information from those who have "been there, done that," so, if you want to help a colleague while also refining your own practice, consider putting pen to paper and sharing what you know.

Learn Long Distance

Don't have the money to bring a UDL-focused speaker to your school? Consider hiring your favorite consultant or author long-distance. Go to that person's website, or contact his or her publisher to figure out your options. As you engage in your research, you may even find that some experts already have web-based content that you can access for free or for a nominal cost.

Be sure that you cast a wide net as you seek a speaker, consultant or coach. Don't limit your search to book authors, university professors, and professional presenters. You might want to look into working with your favorite bloggers or the teachers and teams you read about in professional publications (e.g., *The Journal, Educational Leadership, The Reading Teacher*), for instance.

Pin It

Use Pinterest (www.pinterest.com) to catalog and organize your UDL ideas. Create boards for the tools you use most often (e.g., authentic assessments, Foldables™, cooperative learning structures, centers, tiered lessons, project-based learning, cubed lessons). Pin your favorites and add your own. Share boards with other teachers and administrators.

Pinterest can also be used to communicate with families. Pin your favorite apps, videos, study tips, and learning materials, and provide recommendations on how to use them for homework or at-home study.

This cataloging of ideas has many benefits. It provides a useful resource for all educators in your school or district, and it also serves as a reminder to keep innovating for the person moderating or creating it. Further, it is a way to give and get support and recognition as Pinterest will help you instantly connect to other educators and other classrooms.

Start A Collection

Visit your school's professional library and browse the available books on differentiated instruction, UDL, and teaching diverse learners. Once you have the collection in front of you, do an informal assessment. Are the books current? Do they cover a range of topics (e.g., co-teaching, flipped classrooms, student engagement, brain-based teaching)?

If you feel that the resources are not adequate, start a conversation with your librarian, building principal, or department chair about updating and enhancing the collection.

Be A Learner First

Read and converse professionally. Make UDL easier by connecting with others who are engaged in the same work.

Read professional journals, books, and/or blogs on the topic regularly. Jump on Twitter and start a conversation with fellow teachers. Take the time to discuss ideas with colleagues in your building. Share lesson plans for collegial review. Stay up to date on best practices by attending conferences or professional development on UDL. Observe other teachers as they implement UDL-related strategies in their classrooms. Invite colleagues and administrators who are proficient in UDL to your classroom to observe one or more lessons.

Day 37

Create A Book Club

Does your UDL model need improvement? Start a school-wide book club. Read books about diversity, inclusion, or differentiated instruction. Or, look for titles on teaching supports and techniques related to UDL (e.g., co-teaching, collaboration, community building, learning menus, classroom technology, Professional Learning Communities).

The following are a few texts that make good book club selections:

> Kluth, P. & Danaher, S. (2010). *From talking sticks to tutor sticks: 100 ways to differentiate instruction in K–12 inclusive classrooms.* Baltimore, MD: Paul H. Brookes.

> Kluth, P. & Danaher, S. (2013). *From text maps to memory caps: 100 more ways to differentiate instruction in K–12 inclusive classrooms.* Baltimore, MD: Paul H. Brookes.

> Meyer, A. Rose, D. & Gordon, D. (2014). *Universal design for learning: Theory and practice.* Wakefield, MA: CAST Professional Publishing.

> Novak, K. (2014). *UDL now!: A teacher's Monday morning guide to implementing The Common Core Standards using Universal Design for Learning.* Wakefield, MA: CAST Professional Publishing.

> Novak, K. & Rodriguez, K. (2016). *Universally designed leadership: Applying UDL to systems and schools.* Wakefield, MA: CAST Professional Publishing.

> Ralabate, P. (2016). *Your UDL lesson planner.* Baltimore, MD: Paul H. Brookes.

> Salend, S. (2009). *Classroom testing and assessment for all students: Beyond standardization.* Thousand Oaks, CA: Corwin.

> Tomlinson, C.A. (2014). *The differentiated classroom: Responding to the needs of all learners* (2nd ed.). Alexandria, VA: Association for Supervision and Curriculum Development.

> Udvari-Solner, A. & Kluth, P. (2008). *Joyful learning. Active and collaborative learning in the inclusive classroom.* Thousand Oaks, CA: Corwin Press.

Day 38

Create An Article Club

Don't have time to devote to a book club? Start an article or blog club. Have teachers find provocative journal articles and internet newsletters and discuss them during a designated meeting time (e.g., every Friday during the potluck breakfast in the staff lounge).

Want ideas for getting started? Try these free sites and publications:

> *Current Issues* in Education (cie.asu.edu)

> *Education Next* (educationnext.org)

> *Educational Theory* (education.illinois.edu/educational-theory)

> Edutopia (www.edutopia.org)

> *International Journal of Whole Schooling* (www.wholeschooling.net/Journal_of_Whole_Schooling/IJWSIndex.html)

> National Center on UDL (www.udlcenter.org/resource_library/articles)

> National Education Association (www.nea.org)

Day 39

Create A Tech Club

Don't have time to devote to a book club or even an article club? How about a tech tool club? Choose an app, website, or other tech tool to explore with colleagues. Study it, read about it, experiment with it as a group, and then try it with your students. Reconvene every week or so to provide feedback, updates, reviews, and tips for implementation.

Want ideas for getting started? Try these popular sites and tools:

› Formative (goformative.com)

› Noisli (www.noisli.com)

› Tiki-Toki (www.tiki-toki.com)

› Google Cardboard (vr.google.com/cardboard)

› Ning (www.ning.com)

› e-Pals (www.epals.com)

› emaze (www.emaze.com)

› Write About (www.writeabout.com)

› Versal (www.versal.com)

› StoryboardThat (www.storyboardthat.com)

› CueThink (www.cuethink.com)

› Virtual Nerd (www.virtualnerd.com)

› Classkick (www.classkick.com)

Grab A Coffee

Have a regular coffee date with a colleague interested in UDL. Take turns informally sharing information on topics related to your classroom, your students, and your lessons. To make these meetings as fruitful as possible, consider brainstorming a list of "coffee talk" topics at the beginning of the year. Then, you can browse the list and pick one idea to discuss every time you fill your cups together.

Go Ahead & Brag

If you try something new in your UDL classroom and it is a success, find a way to brag about it to your colleagues. Set aside time at a faculty meeting and give some implementation tips. Offer to hold a brown bag lunch on the strategy. Tweet pictures of the idea and use your school's or district's hashtag so your colleagues see your good work. If you brag a little, your strategies may spread, and others may be inspired to share their own ideas with the group.

Pick Pineapple

Many educators feel that growing their UDL model means learning more, but sometimes, teaching others in the community (or even those far from your community) can be even more helpful than reading another book or attending another seminar.

One way to teach others is to open your doors and invite visitors to tour your school or classroom. Make the experience even richer by offering lunch meetings with willing teachers, and showing video clips that illustrate practices popular at your school (e.g., push-in supports from therapists, project-based instruction).

If you want to formalize this process, create a pineapple chart in your school (Barnes & Gonzalez, 2015). A pineapple chart is a visual that is posted in a faculty lounge and filled with "invitations" to classrooms. When an educator in the building is doing something new or potentially interesting during a given week (e.g., introducing reciprocal teaching, trying exhibitions, using Timetoast), he or she lists it on the chart to let others know when it will happen. Usually the chart is broken into periods or time slots so that every educator can easily see what they can observe second period on Tuesday, for instance.

The pineapple chart is named for a fruit that symbolizes hospitality and the name of the tool really does indicate its purpose. Visitors are welcome and they do not need to do anything more than relax and observe. These pop-ins are not about evaluating or even providing feedback to a colleague. Teachers come and stay for just a few minutes or an entire lesson. It is as casual as it is potentially powerful.

Day 43

Find Me On Facebook

Are you on Facebook? Do you visit the site on a regular basis? If so, click on over to my page to learn even more about UDL, inclusive education, and designing classroom experiences for all (**www.facebook.com/paulakluth**).

Explore all of the resources I have posted including photographs of classroom ideas, helpful video clips, teaching tips, and remarks and advice from other educators.

Join me today. Let's keep the conversation going!

Practice What You Preach

Ask your administrator to highlight or even demonstrate a new UDL technique at each faculty meeting. This practice not only helps other teachers learn new ideas, but will also potentially jazz up your meetings. Instead of showing off your new disc seat cushions, let some of your colleagues use them during the meeting. Don't talk about a new brain break, try it out with the group to get everyone inspired to learn at the end of a long day. And if you want to praise the use of visuals, use them during the meeting; distribute an infographic-style agenda to the group and create a presentation filled with photos and clever diagrams.

Talk With TED

TED Talks are popular because they help us think differently about the world and our work. These short clips can serve as pick-me-ups when you are seeking motivation for supporting learners in your UDL classroom:

› *How to Fix a Broken School* by Linda Cliatt-Wayman
   www.ted.com/talks/linda_cliatt_wayman_how_to_fix_a_broken_school_lead_fearlessly_love_hard

› *Hey Science Teachers—Make It Fun!* by Tyler DeWitt
   www.ted.com/talks/tyler_dewitt_hey_science_teachers_make_it_fun?language=en

› *Teach Teachers How to Create Magic* by Christopher Emdin
   www.ted.com/talks/christopher_emdin_teach_teachers_how_to_create_magic?language=en

› *3 Rules to Spark Learning* by Ramsey Musallam
   www.ted.com/talks/ramsey_musallam_3_rules_to_spark_learning?language=en

› *Do Schools Kill Creativity?* by Sir Ken Robinson
   www.ted.com/talks/ken_robinson_says_schools_kill_creativity

› *How to Escape Education's Death Valley* by Sir Ken Robinson
   www.ted.com/talks/ken_robinson_how_to_escape_education_s_death_valley

Set UDL Goals

Want to be successful in your commitment to reaching all students? Try setting specific UDL-focused goals that will keep you accountable and serve as a tool for motivation. Here are some examples:

> I will try one new enrichment strategy by January 15, 2017.

> I will recruit and train three classroom volunteers for math stations by January 31, 2017.

> I will use at least six new active learning techniques to enhance my lectures by March 1, 2017.

> I will co-teach three lessons with our reading specialist by April 30, 2017.

> I will use cubing in three different science lessons. I will do this monthly throughout the 2017/2018 school year.

> I will teach my classroom paraprofessional about UDL by September 1, 2017.

> I will attend one UDL workshop or seminar by November 30, 2017.

Day 47

Get The Word Out

Don't keep the information in this book to yourself. Share it to create change in your department, grade level, or school.

Post the tips on your school's website. Make posters featuring some of these ideas and plaster your staff lounge, restrooms, or meeting rooms. Choose one idea and email it to your colleagues each week. Tear the pages out and use them to wallpaper an area of your office meeting room.

You can also use this book in a more collaborative way. Have every teacher in your department, building, or district choose a handful of ideas from these pages, try them out, and report back to colleagues with a review.

Put Them On A Panel

Organize a panel discussion with a few teachers in your building or district who are enthusiastic and successful practitioners of differentiation and/or Universal Design for Learning techniques. Have each present a few ideas and then open the session up to Q & A. This could take place for an hour after school, or for a longer period of time during a formal professional development event.

Go To The Fair

Sure, you've been to a fair, but have you been to a UDL fair? If not, put it on your bucket list and start planning.

To put on a fair, ask teachers in your building to bring examples of universally-designed curriculum, instruction, and assessment to the staff lounge. Then take all of these submissions and arrange them into different displays so that like materials are grouped together and educators can compare their ideas to similar ideas shared by colleagues.

You can sort materials by subject area. You can also set up displays based on the UDL categories and assemble materials related to

› methods of representation (e.g., primary sources, visual directions),

› methods of action and expression (e.g., portfolios, interactive notebooks), and

› methods of engagement (e.g., journals, choice boards).

Then, invite teachers to visit the staff lounge at any time during the exhibit, including during their lunch period. You might even add in a raffle to encourage them to spend more time with the materials and to create an opportunity to give away books, teaching tools, and resources related to UDL.

Workshop It

Sometimes the best way to learn new skills is to get out of the building, connect with like-minded educators, and assume the role of student. Look for workshops offered in your area on topics related to UDL such as co-teaching, collaborative learning, culturally-relevant teaching, authentic assessment, literature circles, drama in the classroom, blended learning, and using choice menus.

Don't forget to take a colleague or administrator along so you can talk about the content and plan for ways to implement new ideas when you get back to school.

Day 51

Blog All About It

Need to get out of a rut? At a loss for fresh ideas? Feeling isolated? Connecting with other teachers with similar goals may be just what you need. There are plenty of teacher blogs on the internet, with more surfacing every day. There are blogs specifically dedicated to UDL, differentiated instruction, Response to Intervention (RTI), inclusive education, and other related topics.

Blogs can help and inspire teachers in a variety of ways. For starters, they provide a sense of connectedness. If you don't have a lot of support to reach your UDL-related goals, blogs can provide a community. They are also a source of new ideas. Busy bloggers have opportunities to create, document, and reflect constantly. The thoughts and products they share can be invaluable. Finally, teacher-bloggers are often accessible in ways that a textbook author or seminar speaker may not be; therefore, you can do more than passively learn from a blogger. You can often interact with both the blogger and his or her followers.

There are many ways to find the best blogs for your needs. You may want to start with Teach.com, and check out their blog ranking system, The Teach100 (teach.com/teach100). You can also check the Edublog Awards (edublogawards.com) for the annual list of best blogs in categories ranging from Best Administrator Blog, to Best Teacher Blog, to Best Ed Tech Blog.

Who knows? After a lot of blog reading, you may want to create your own teacher blog, which is a great way to learn while you teach, and get feedback on the hard work you do day in and day out.

UDL Your Own PD

The principles of UDL are undoubtedly important in the classroom, but they are important for the staff room, too. Just as lessons need to fit the needs, strengths, and interests of learners, professional development should respond to teachers as individuals.

Seek out a range of ways to educate yourself about UDL. Maybe you love reading short and to-the-point books like this one, and want to grab a single daily idea to keep your practice on track. If so, look for other resources in this format and keep them on hand as you plan and work in the classroom.

But what if reading isn't your favorite way to get information? That's okay! Just seek out other ways to learn about flipping the classroom, using projects, and varying your teaching strategies. Join a webinar, ask administrators to send you to a workshop, observe other teachers with a lot of experience with universal design, or ask your principal if there is someone in the district available to serve as your UDL coach for a period of time. You can also customize your professional development by engaging in a mix of these activities.

Section II

Teaching & Learning with UDL

Methods of Engagement

Start A Conversation

Looking for a new way to encourage both listening and sharing? Try conversation circles.

To create circles, put students into groups of four. Then, provide a prompt (e.g., "Who are the heroes in *To Kill a Mockingbird*?") and have one student begin answering the question. After about a minute, sound a bell or chime to indicate that a second person should begin talking. The second student will immediately pick up where the first student left off, building on his or her answer. The process continues until every student has made a contribution.

Discuss Discussions

Some students need supports to participate in classroom discussions. You may need to ensure that some learners and/or groups have choices in where they sit or meet to increase their comfort. You may also want to provide group norms to help students understand how to interact effectively with others. In addition, you might consider

> asking students to draft a list of questions for discussion;

> providing a list of sentence stems to help students frame statements, interact collaboratively, and state their thoughts clearly;

> modeling interpersonal and interdependence skills in advance (e.g., active listening);

> assigning roles, so everyone can participate in different ways;

> programing students' communication devices with any necessary words or phrases;

> giving groups concrete tasks to accomplish; and

> varying the size, seating, or composition of discussion groups as needed.

Start With Students

Customize content by using student-generated questions. As you introduce a unit or lesson ask your students what they already know about the topic and have them work with classmates to discuss what they want to know about it. Have them create posters to document their discussions. Keep these visuals up in the classroom so they can be referenced during lessons and throughout the unit. Make these products interactive by having students add sticky notes, pictures, doodles, and even QR codes to them throughout the unit as their questions are answered. These visuals then become tools for both learning and review.

Methods of Engagement

Talk About It

What better way to work on a range of skills than to stage a talk show and channel Oprah, Ellen, and Jimmy Fallon?

Put one or more students in the role of host. Then, assign others to roles as celebrities, book characters, famous writers, historical figures, or renowned scientists.

You may have to structure the activity to make sure that all students can participate successfully. For example, you might give your guests a form detailing facts about their life, personal viewpoints, and positions on topics. This page can then serve as a cheat sheet during the interviews. You can also create a script for the host so that the guests know which questions might be asked. To make the show worthwhile viewing, and to be sure that students are exposed to key content, you might share relevant video clips in between guest interviews. Just as all talk show hosts play footage from their guests' movies and television shows to promote their work, your host can share videos related to his or her subject's area of expertise. An interview with the Wright brothers, for instance, might feature a clip of their 1909 test flight from History.com.

Talk shows are great for presenting content in an attention-grabbing way, but also for allowing students to polish or demonstrate skills. Some students may need to work on speaking in an audible voice, or using a new augmentative communication system, and may, therefore, be assigned a role as announcer. Another student may be an excellent researcher and could be put in the role of gathering background on guests and feeding them details when needed.

Day 57

Write On The Furniture

Want to give personalized feedback? Cover student desks with dry erase paper so you can leave them notes. Provide remarks about their effort, their progress, and their accomplishments (e.g., "Your notebook is complete-amazing diagrams!").

You can also use the desks to

› share compliments (e.g., "Proud of your participation in the Geography Bee last night"),

› provide reminders (e.g., "Reread Chapter 7 by tomorrow"),

› give study tips (e.g., "Get a good night's sleep tonight!"),

› cheer them on (e.g., "So glad you are back today!"), and

› thank them (e.g., "Thanks for bringing CJ her homework! What a friend!").

If you like this idea and your students are responding positively to it, consider other ways to connect with them. You might, for instance, put sticky notes of encouragement on their lockers or even mail them postcards with information on their progress in your classroom.

Day 58

Add To Assess

Menus are a popular form of assessment in the UDL classroom. There are several different types we can offer students, but one of the most straightforward is what is called a tally menu. To make one, create a list of activities related to course content, and assign each one of these activities a point value. Then, tell your learners they must accumulate a certain number of points to successfully complete the unit. This allows them to learn in a variety of ways and to make choices based on their interests and strengths. Hopefully, it also inspires creativity and encourages some students to invent their own ways of mastering content and skills.

Directions

Complete as many activities as you wish. You must submit materials/activities worth at least 50 points.

I completed	activities	points
	Read *The Great Kapok Tree* and create a book trailer for it.	25
	Engage in a mini-lesson with Mr. H.	10
	Create a 3-D diagram of the layers of the rain forest.	25
	Make a rain forest fact infographic.	15
	Your choice: Discuss your idea with one of your teachers and have them initial here _____ before beginning work.	10-50

# of points: _____

Sculpt, Sew & Assemble

It's time to get creative!

Collaborative art projects like murals, large sculptures, mosaics, and quilts are perfect projects for diverse groups of students, as everyone can participate. Usually, there are many different roles and ways for students to contribute. For example, one or two students might facilitate the production of a mosaic, as others do the designing and assembling.

Keep in mind that these projects can be created outside of the art classroom. A social studies teacher may have students create a memorial sculpture for the community, and a science teacher might have his classes create a mural exploring a concept or an area of study such as ecology or microbiology.

Day 60 Turn & Talk

A low-prep way to provide engagement opportunities for all students is to implement a "turn and talk" technique. At certain intervals in a lecture or whole-class discussion, ask students to turn to the person next to them and discuss the content that has just been presented. To make the exercise even more purposeful, you might give them a specific prompt. For instance:

› Ask your partner a question about _____.

› Make a prediction about _____.

› Draw one thing I just taught and tell your partner about the illustration.

› Share something I presented that was surprising/interesting/confusing.

› Teach your partner what I just presented.

› Define a vocabulary word I used in the first 15 minutes of this lecture.

This technique gives students opportunities to process what they are learning, and to work on collaborative behaviors such as asking clarifying questions, paraphrasing, and turn-taking.

Go Beyond The Book Report

Giving choices and alternatives to "the ways things are done around here" is not only a UDL strategy, but a way to encourage students to demonstrate new skills and competencies. For instance, some students may like the decades-old practice of writing book reports, but others will appreciate having options for demonstrating learning and communicating comprehension. Allow these students to

> create a Facebook page or Twitter account for three characters;

> write a series of letters between two characters;

> create a scrapbook, memory box, or Instagram page that a main character might have made;

> participate in a panel discussion with others who read the book;

> create a soundtrack for the book;

> develop a podcast about the book;

> make a diorama;

> create book illustrations for each chapter;

> make a cartoon strip or graphic novel retelling the story;

> make a mind map of the entire book;

> create an illustrated timeline of events;

> write a piece of fan fiction; or

> engage in a group performance of a "deleted scene" from the book.

Add your own ideas to this list and have students do the same. Then, consider other assignments for which you might create alternatives. Research papers? Lab notes? Spelling tests?

Introduce A Bill

Trying to teach how a bill becomes a law? Try a simulation. Let students take on roles representing the three branches of government. Have them write bills, introduce the bills to their classmates, vote on bills proposed by others, and wait to see which ones pass and make it to the opposite house of Congress.

This type of simulation has many benefits in a diverse classroom. It helps educators dive deeper into the content, provides students with opportunities to practice communication and social skills, and often inspires learning beyond the classroom and the textbook.

You can create simulations to teach many different types of content, including

›   historical events (e.g., Cuban Missile Crisis, Exxon Oil Spill),

›   political processes (e.g., electing a president, becoming a U.S. citizen), and

›   problem-solving situations (e.g., dealing with bullying, providing CPR after an accident).

Go Hunting

Looking for a new lesson idea to get you out of the room or even the school? A scavenger hunt is an easy-to-implement learning activity that encourages creativity and collaboration. Further, it can be easily differentiated by providing different challenges to separate groups, or by giving personal support and coaching to some learners or groups.

To create a scavenger hunt for the classroom, create a list of directions (e.g., "Find an acute angle"; "Find an example of intersecting lines"; "Find something that is at least one cubic foot in size") and have students search the classroom, playground, building, or surrounding neighborhood to complete the assigned tasks.

You can pair them up with partners for this exercise or let them work in small groups of three or four. To provide even more support for this activity, you might assign a few students to function as "hunt helpers"; the function of these individuals is to give clues and guide students to resources.

Day 64

Skim & Stick

Get your group ready to read with this simple collaborative strategy. Give each student a handful of sticky notes. Then set a timer for about five minutes and ask them to place the notes on what appear to be the most interesting parts of a chapter or book. You can be very general with your directions or a bit more specific. You could, for instance, ask students to put a green sticky note on a striking piece of dialogue, or a red note on an illustration, diagram, or image they want to explore further.

At the end of the exercise, have students share their selections with a partner. As they share, make your way around the classroom and take notes on the passages students chose. This information can then be used during the formal study of the material. For instance, if a few students seemed captivated by a certain monologue in the book, you can point this out during a discussion of that passage, and ask those particular students to share their thoughts with the group.

Methods of Engagement

Keep A Journal

Journals are flexible learning tools that can be used at any grade level and across many subject areas. They work well as a daily comprehension check, springboards for future discussions, or tools for investigation, observation, or reflection.

There are as many uses for journals as there are students in your classroom. You can page through them on occasion as an informal assessment, ask students to use them as conversation starters, or "borrow" excerpts to share on a classroom website or Twitter account.

While journals are often used as class startup activities, they can actually be inserted anywhere in a lesson. Introduce them mid-lecture to get all learners to respond to points you have just outlined. Use them at the end of a lesson to help students unpack what they have just learned. Or, have students engage in "bookend" journaling as a way to record their impressions at the beginning and end of a lesson (e.g., "What does healthy eating mean to you?" and "How have your views changed about healthy eating after today's discussion on processed foods?").

Students can be asked to create any number of different entries in their journals including

> sketches, pictures, or diagrams;

> reflections;

> brainstorming;

> graphic organizers; and

> "graffiti lists" using various fonts, shapes, and colors.

Freeze That Frame

Want to add a bit of novelty to your next lesson? Try tableau. If your students have not had much exposure to drama, it is a perfect first taste as there are many ways to contribute and participate, and very few rules.

In tableau, participants use their bodies to make still images. These images represent a scene, word, concept, idea, or theme. It can be used to explore a particular moment in a story or novel (especially useful when many characters are involved), to replicate a painting or photograph, to replay and "visit" a historical moment, or to illustrate or visually define a word or concept. For instance, students might create images of different ways to think about negative numbers, vocabulary words like *objectify* and *random*, various scenes from *The Year of the Boar & Jackie Robinson*, significant moments in space travel, or interpretations of Ellis Wilson's *Funeral Procession*.

Since there is no movement or speaking allowed, a tableau is easier to manage than a whole-group improvisation, yet it can easily lead into extended drama activities.

Start A Snowball

Looking for a response structure that provides a little peer support for those who struggle to work independently? Try this "snowball" activity that encourages listening, synthesis of ideas, and collaboration.

Provide a prompt or question to the group (e.g., "What is the study of algebra?"; "Defend Truman's decision to drop the atomic bomb"). Have every student create a written response to the question. After a few minutes, have students find a partner and compare their responses. Then, direct them to combine content with their partner and create a new collaborative response using elements from both of their initial responses.

Keep the snowball going with groups of four and—if time permits—groups of eight.

Finally, bring students together to talk about the final products they created and to discuss the "snowball" process. Specifically, you might ask them what they learned from working as a team and how their understanding of the material changed as they revised their responses.

Study The Standards

In the beginning of the year (and from unit to unit) it can be really helpful to explicitly explain the purpose of learning standards to your students.

Share not only the "what" of the standards, but also the "why" and the "how" of teaching and learning them. Then, break the class into small groups and assign each one a standard. Have the groups make posters illustrating the standard, present ideas for meeting the standard, and suggest activities and even lessons related to the standard.

Temporarily post these visuals around the room, and let students know you will be taking their ideas into consideration as you plan.

Define Success

Continually share criteria for success with your students. In other words, don't make them guess what they will need to do, provide, or show to achieve at a high level in your classroom.

What goals do they need to meet? What skills do they need to demonstrate? Are there attitudes, mindsets, and work behaviors you want them to cultivate? Are they expected to contribute to the classroom community in certain ways? Let them know exactly what is expected, and encourage them to exceed those expectations.

Other ideas for defining success include

> paraphrasing the learning target;

> using checklists, rubrics, and graphic organizers to illustrate expectations;

> referring to the lesson goal or target when providing feedback;

> developing and displaying anchor charts; and

> introducing exemplars.

Focus On Photos

They say a picture is worth a thousand words. Put that theory to the test today by giving students opportunities to show what they know using only a camera.

Break the class into small groups and charge them with illustrating a piece of content (e.g., vocabulary word, theme from a novel, theory) by shooting and sharing a collection of photographs. If students need only take two or three photos, verbal directions may suffice, but if you want them to complete a longer project (e.g., illustrating five different poems), be sure to provide a checklist so groups can keep track of each image as it is captured.

Give them some time to discuss the challenge and plan their photos, and then cut them loose to set up and take their pictures. Students can either take pictures of what they see or they can stage photos that include fellow students, objects, props, and visuals/signage.

When everyone has finished taking their snaps, give each group a bit of time to show off their work. Use the images to start a discussion and potentially to inspire another round of picture taking.

Jump On A Raft

A RAFT isn't just a flotation device; it's also a popular writing strategy!

RAFT stands for ROLE, AUDIENCE, FORMAT, and TOPIC. To use one in the classroom, assign a TOPIC such as, "Defend your participation in a food chain." Then, give students options for creatively demonstrating their understanding of that topic using any number of roles (e.g., doctor, author), audiences (e.g., teenagers, football fans), and formats (e.g., free verse, bulleted list). So, a student might write from the ROLE of a great white shark to the AUDIENCE of humans using a FORMAT of a "Top 10 List" to defend their participation in the food chain (e.g., 1. I help to control the seal population; 2. I eat the sick and keep prey populations healthy).

RAFT is a popular strategy in UDL classrooms because teachers can use it to address many goals at once. It also presents opportunities to provide choice, which is one of the easiest ways to individualize instruction. Finally, it allows learners to tackle different assignments based on their needs, interests, or abilities. For example, you can ask some students to create multi-step letters, and others to produce drawings, cartoons, lists, or photo essays.

Day 72

Assemble The Puzzle

Jigsaw (Kagan, 1989) is a structure that allows students to learn a lot of content in a short amount of time. It lets learners polish their teaching skills and collaborate with peers. It also gives every student in the classroom an opportunity to serve as an expert.

To start a jigsaw in your classroom, assemble small groups of students. These constellations are called "base groups."

Students in each base group are given a multifaceted topic to explore. Each member of the group selects one piece on which to focus. So, if the topic is simple machines, one student might be focused on lever, one on pulley, one on inclined plane, and so on. All base groups should split their content up in the same way. That is, each group should delegate responsibilities so that all the machines are being studied and each group member is taking responsibility for just one of them.

Every student in the classroom is responsible for learning enough about his or her topic to be able to teach that content to the rest of his or her base group. Students engage in this part of the work with their "expert group"; this group consists of all of the students who have the same assignment. That is, all of the students assigned to learn about the inclined plane will meet, research, gather information, and become experts on the topic.

When students in the expert groups feel that they have thoroughly learned their portion of the material, they plan a few strategies and perhaps even create materials for teaching it to their base groups. Students then move back to those base groups and teach their lessons. In this way, all of the students in the classroom learn all of the material.

Day 73

Write Around

In a UDL classroom, you are often teaching students to be resourceful. This activity emphasizes that skill and also serves as a unique way to dive into new content or review something that has just been presented.

To begin, put students in small groups, and ask them to sit in a circle formation. Direct all of them to write an open-ended problem or question on the top of their papers (e.g., "How do you cope with stress?"). Each student in the group then passes their paper to the classmate on his or her right.

Students immediately begin answering the questions on the papers. After a few minutes, use a chime or bell to signal them to pass their papers once again. Repeat until every group member has answered every question.

When you finish the exercise, have students discuss questions and answers in small groups, or direct them to engage in a follow-up activity. For example, they might graph the responses they received, or use the material as the basis for an essay.

Day 74

Survey Students

Distribute an informal assessment a few times a year to get feedback. Focus questions on needs, strengths, and student ideas. For example:

> What do you want to learn this/next/by the end of the year?

> What do you need to be comfortable in my classroom?

> What was your favorite lesson so far?

> What do you like most/least about our classroom space?

> Who do you like working with the most? Who do you work with most effectively?

> What games/structures/activities do you like best and why?

> What is one thing you have learned so far in this class?

These questions will help you individualize instruction and get to know your students a little better.

Get Out The Tri-Folds

When adults recall the most memorable learning experiences from their school days, many of them talk about projects. Who doesn't have a memory of creating something, hauling materials from home to school, and engaging in "real work" like research, design, and investigation?

Teachers working in multi-level classrooms often turn to projects in order to provide interesting and appropriate instruction for all, and to make sure that students have opportunities to pursue individual learning objectives in the context of daily instruction. Students without identified needs can work on organizing time and materials, writing for new audiences, or polishing interviewing skills, and students with disabilities might practice those same skills while also honing communication or social competencies (e.g., asking for help, giving clear directions). All of these skills can be addressed as students tackle the same or similar projects and access challenging content.

Project ideas are literally endless and might include

> building a model,

> collecting community stories,

> creating a podcast,

> writing a one-act play,

> inventing a game or toy, and

> designing an app.

Rap Around

Wrap up today's learning with a rap around. Use this structure to end a lesson or a unit. It will give you a snapshot of student understanding of a concept, idea, or standard, and allow learners to build on the perspectives of others.

To use it, put students in groups of three and ask them to take turns, sharing

› something memorable about the lesson,

› a question about the lesson, and

› one to three words related to the lesson.

The prompts are to be shared one at a time, so direct learners to answer the first prompt during the first round, the second during the second round, and the third during the final round. Everyone, therefore, shares something they found memorable about the lesson before the group moves on to the second prompt.

Book It

There are so many reasons to use book clubs in your UDL classroom. First of all, book clubs expose students to authors and genres they might not choose on their own. Second of all, they give students opportunities to learn about events, people, and phenomena through different voices and perspectives. Finally, this structure encourages student ownership over reading (Kluth & Chandler-Olcott, 2007).

According to O'Donnell-Allen (2006), book clubs should have these characteristics:

› They are made up of small groups of readers.

› They engage in systematic discussion.

› They discuss books (and other texts) of the members' choice.

› They use a variety of open-ended response methods (e.g., journal entries, graphic organizers) to prompt extended discussion.

› Membership varies according to the desired configuration.

Perhaps the best aspect of the book club is that it can accommodate students with any number of different needs, strengths, and abilities. Students can choose the book they want to read, they can be assigned a range of different roles (e.g., word wizard, story mapper), and they can use various learning supports, such as e-readers, story maps, and highlighters to access the material.

Build Community

Students of all ages have to feel safe, empowered, and connected in order to work effectively. They need opportunities to share with others, learn from peers, and give and get support.

There are many ways to build community in the classroom. You can involve students in conversations about collaboration, select materials that reinforce messages of support, and emphasize practices that build social skills.

You can also use community-building games that enhance relationships in the classroom, encourage friendships, and foster student-to-student learning opportunities. Use them in August and September and look for opportunities to continue to integrate them into your lessons throughout the year. Games that can be used across grade levels include

> scavenger hunts,

> charades,

> two truths and a lie,

> twenty questions, and

> one-minute stories.

Get Ready, Get Set & Get Writing

If you want to bring the excitement of the sporting arena into the classroom, introduce this playful competition to your learners.

Divide your students into teams and have them "speed share" responses to a prompt or question (e.g., "List facts about Ancient Egypt"; "Share the questions you have about snakes"; "What are some symbols used in *Lord of the Flies?*"). Once they have the topic, set a timer, and let them go to work.

Be sure to remind students of a few simple guidelines:

› Include every group member in the activity.

› Use more than one scribe to get more answers on the page.

› Keep voices low so that the scribes in each group can easily hear their own group members.

You can invite students to write for a short period of time and use this activity as an energizer or you can give them 10 or 20 minutes and use it as a review for an upcoming assessment.

At the end of a set period of time, have students share their answers. Students' responses can also be shared on a classroom blog or even pinned to a classroom bulletin board.

Be Goal Oriented

Understand that some students will have different lesson goals than others. Most students in most lessons will be addressing the same targets as their peers during daily lessons, but if your school is truly diverse and you are supporting those with a wide range of needs in your classroom, you will have occasionally have different students focused on different goals. For example, during a lesson on demonstration speeches in a middle school language arts classroom, a student who struggles to speak might be working on the goal of accessing his augmentative communication system to share remarks with the class. While others are being assessed on their posture, pace, and inflection, this learner might be assessed on his ability to stand in front of the group and navigate the dynamic menu on his device.

Inspire Wonder

Put inquiry at the center of classroom learning. Focus on student interests, questions, and curiosities throughout the days, weeks, and months of the school year.

There are many ways to make your classroom a place of wonder. You might:

› Model wonder. Talk about your own questions, passions, and interests. Discuss your own quests.

› Share your methods for learning more and exploring new topics.

› Check out Wonderopolis (www.wonderopolis.org) to find materials for making an interactive wonder jar, a store of items related to questions and learning, and a "wonder of the day."

› Bring interesting materials, artifacts, and images into the classroom. Put out a model of the human ear while you teach about the human body. Post a series of current political cartoons during an election year. Adopt a class pet to encourage observation and questions.

› Share questions and encourage interaction using a digital collaboration tool such as Padlet (www.padlet.com) or TodaysMeet (www.todaysmeet.com).

› Give inquiry a home. Introduce the language of wonder to your students. Create a space in the classroom dedicated to the practice of asking questions. Have a "wonder time" each month where students take turns asking and answering questions. Post questions on the classroom door. Introduce a wonder hashtag (e.g., #Room101Wonders; #MathMondayMusings) for your learning community to use.

Offer The Almanac

Make sure that there is something for everybody in your classroom library. This means offering many different genres (e.g., humor, reference) and including materials that all students can read or explore independently. This also means considering the unique needs and preferences of your students. Some students read only magazines and comic books. Others are only beginning to learn English and will want materials in Spanish, Japanese, Polish, Chinese, Russian, Arabic, Tagalog or other languages. Still others may have very specific interests. Some students on the autism spectrum—and likely others without identified needs—enjoy reading catalogs, almanacs, and even advertisements, for instance.

Play Tic-Tac-Toe

Tic-tac-toe boards are a must for the UDL classroom, as they allow every learner to study the material in a completely unique way while addressing the same unit goals or lesson objectives.

Different teachers have different rules for using tic-tac-toe boards, but most ask students to complete three tasks diagonally, down a column, or across a row. Some teachers require all students to use the middle square so that there will be one common assignment in the unit.

To create your tic-tac-toe board, identify the outcomes and instructional focus of a unit of study. Then, use data, observations, conversations with learners, and student profiles to determine the learning styles and interests in your classroom. Finally, design nine different tasks that will both address lesson goals and honor student learning needs.

Keep in mind that there are many ways to make tic-tac-toe more or less complex. For instance, you might let students work in teams, challenge some of them to complete all the tasks, or keep one square open for any learner wanting to customize an activity based on personal interests.

Day 84

Get Real

Many students are drawn to activities that focus on local or world events. Therefore, you will want to regularly provide students with content that relates to individual interests, while still connecting them to standards-based content. Use television, movies, music, news stories, and sporting events as inspiration for curriculum and instruction. Let students solve real problems instead of those they find online or in textbooks. Ask them to look around the school, their communities, and the classroom for authentic tasks to tackle.

Cue The Actors

Make your classroom into a stage today and introduce a round or two of Reader's Theater.

Students participating in this structure read directly from scripts to tell a story. They read without props, costumes, or sets, but are encouraged to use intonation, facial expression, prosody, and gestures appropriate to their characters and their characters' words. The scripts are typically created from grade-level books or stories. There are several examples available online including at Teaching Heart (www.teachingheart.net/readerstheater.htm) and the website of Dr. Chase Young (www.thebestclass.org/rtscripts.html).

Reader's Theater is a valuable tool for educators in any classroom, but may be especially useful to those teaching in diverse, inclusive, or even multi-age classrooms because it gives students opportunities to work on social and communication goals (e.g., taking turns, using new signs or gestures, speaking in complete sentences), while they get reading fluency practice, learn new vocabulary words, and strengthen comprehension skills.

There are many different ways to use Reader's Theater in the classroom. You can use it to bring a poem, passage, or chapter alive. You can also use it to break a longer piece of text down into shorter segments to make it more comprehensible. Or you can use this technique to assess comprehension; to engage in this version of the strategy, have students create the scripts themselves so they have to select which ideas, phrases, and words in the text are the most relevant and meaningful.

Make It Mysterious

Get students curious about new learning by giving them mystery envelopes to open at the beginning of a lesson. Fill your envelopes with words, pictures, and small objects. Have students work in groups to solve the mystery and determine what the new area of study will be.

You can ask them to explore and discuss the words in the envelope to start. Then, have students talk about the photos and any objects enclosed. Finally, come together as a whole class, talk about their predictions, and solve the mystery by sharing the new topic and the rationale for each item in the envelope.

To make this more challenging or less complex for certain learners, you can either vary the envelopes so that groups get one of two or three available sets, or you can simply provide some items in each envelope that will present a particular challenge, and one or two that will be easier to interpret.

Day 87

Focus On Feedback

Feedback is an essential part of learning, so be sure your students are getting as much as possible from your guidance, comments, and support (Wiggins, 2012). Start by connecting your feedback to a goal, when possible, as in, "The song should make the audience feel something. It should be an emotional experience. How can you add some heart to the performance?" or "As people visit your station at the science fair, you want to not only have a high-quality project to share, but you also want it to be compelling. You want people to learn and to be interested. How do you think you are doing so far on that goal?"

Another element of effective feedback is making sure it is clear. Telling a learner to "add details" may mean nothing to that individual until they see a few sample essays with details highlighted in neon marker. A student told to "follow through" on their golf swing may have no clue what that means until they see some videos of positive and negative examples.

Finally, high-quality feedback is timely. When work is returned weeks after students have submitted it, the feedback is often totally ignored because it can feel disconnected from the "here and now." When feedback is received very quickly, however, it is better understood and can be immediately responded to as new work is produced. In order to give all students the best feedback possible, try to give it on-the-spot using mini-conferences and by making comments during observations. You can also provide more immediate feedback by enlisting the support of others. Have students work collaboratively to get and give feedback. Bring in classroom volunteers to support projects. Work with partners like therapists, administrators, and literacy specialists on certain tasks. Finally, you can offer well-timed feedback by using tech tools to share comments with individuals (e.g., Google Docs) or with a whole group (e.g., www.yammer.com).

Universal Design Daily © 2017 Paula Kluth

Methods of Engagement

Meet For A Minute

No student wants to hear, "See me for a minute after class." When short teacher meetings are the norm in a classroom and all students are asked to participate in a few of them during the year, however, this practice can promote learning and build classroom connections at the same time.

Minute meetings should, of course, be fairly short and might be held to share

› feedback on work,

› a recommendation,

› an observation,

› encouragement, or

› a question.

If you can't grab students during passing times, try scheduling meetings while the rest of the class is working independently.

Day 89

Innovate

If you have read Daniel Pink's popular book *Drive* (2011), you know about companies that encourage employees to spend a portion of their time engaging in projects of their choice. In some places, Pink reports, workers are encouraged to spend as much as 20 percent of their time on these projects.

Teacher-blogger Josh Stumpenhorst wrote about using this idea in schools. For one day, sixth graders in his school were allowed to focus on any activity they deemed worthy, interesting, or meaningful. This is UDL and then some. Not only did learners have choices in how they spent their time, but they could also work collaboratively and focus on areas of personal interest or skill.

Some of the projects students chose included

> creating a Rube Goldberg machine,

> writing and performing a comedy routine,

> choreographing a dance,

> producing a highlight reel of basketball moves,

> building a model of the Eiffel Tower, and

> writing a short story.

Want to learn more about these types of learning experiences? Read Josh Stumpenhorst's aforementioned post on the topic (www. stumpteacher.com/2011/03/innovation-day-2011.html) and then explore Chris Kesler's retired but content-rich site on how to support students to work on "passion projects" on a weekly basis: www.geniushour.com.

Methods of Engagement

Create Obstacles

If you feel your students are in need of a challenge, plan a lesson filled with obstacles. An obstacle course lesson is a playful way to get students moving, talking, sharing, and laughing.

Start by chunking your lesson into three or four pieces. Then, assign different parts of the lesson to different parts of the room to provide students with opportunities to move and interact with both their peers and a variety of materials. Finally, create obstacles (e.g., brain breaks, mental puzzles) for students to complete between lesson tasks. So, you might begin by having students sit at their desks to solve a few math problems. When they have finished, direct them to move to a corner of the room to get instructions for the next task. The second task might be 10 jumping jacks. You might then have them stay in the corner and read a short passage from the math textbook before moving to another corner of the classroom. Here, you could ask them to engage in a three-step handshake with a partner before sitting down to write a story problem with him or her. And so on.

If you want to level this activity a bit, you can vary the tasks in each area with some students receiving more challenging work assignments than others.

Day 91

Make It Work

Create a classroom that not only works well, but feels predictable and, therefore, safe to many students. Introduce strategies that help students understand what they need to do and when they need to do it. Start with a clear visual schedule of the day's activities. Teachers in elementary schools should post an hour-by-hour summary, and educators in middle school and high school should share at least a general schedule of events for each class period, even if the activities are not listed alongside a time frame. Other tools that will help with the goal of predictability include:

> a monthly and/or annual calendar marked with special days (e.g., birthdays), upcoming events, and deadlines;

> an "FYI" space or designated area of the dry erase board that features current homework assignments and important reminders;

> charts that help students track important information and goals (e.g., progress on the group's 200-book challenge);

> transition cues (e.g., songs to signal the end of group work time); and

> timers (for students to use in independent work and for teachers to project during lessons).

Tour The Museum

Why pay admission to get immersed in history, science, culture, or art when your students can create a museum-like experience right in your classroom?

As a way to begin or end a unit, or just to make learning a little livelier, have students create museum exhibits related to course content. First, determine your theme (e.g., voting, French-speaking nations, habitats). Then, instruct students to gather or create artifacts related to the theme. Finally, have them add captions or other helpful visuals to their displays.

When students finish their exhibits, have them serve as docents or guides and invite visitors (e.g., other classes, families, local seniors, building staff, teachers) to the museum.

Ask The Experts

Most teachers have been in the position of struggling to figure out a new tech tool or piece of equipment. The response of most educators is to send for tech support. In most schools, there is only one person in this role. Therefore, teachers and their students may not be able to get the help they need when they need it.

Fortunately, there is an elegant solution to this problem. Teachers can turn to their students for support. You may not be able to get much help from very young children, but those in upper elementary grades, middle school, and high school may be able to offer quite a bit of support.

Survey your students to learn about their tech-related interests and abilities. Use this process to find experts on Prezi, Keynote, PowToon, Google Drive, WordPress, Glogster, Diigo, Dropbox, Twitter, PicMonkey, Canvas, Edmodo, Evernote, Skype, Storybird, Pinterest, YouTube, StoryJumper, Picktochart, and more. You can ask these students to help out when needed. You can also look for opportunities to highlight their skills during lessons. Bring experts forward to co-teach as new tools are introduced. Or, you can take a few minutes each week to allow one or two students to teach or discuss favorite tools, apps, and websites.

Move Higher In The Hierarchy

Instead of asking students to simply answer questions, have them evaluate, analyze, or compare. That is, throw out a few HOT (Higher Order Thinking) questions. HOT questions provide students with the tools to think and assess. They also can make classroom concepts feel or appear more meaningful or relevant, and help students learn new vocabulary.

To construct your questions, it may help to examine the levels of Bloom's Revised Taxonomy (Anderson, Krathwohl, Airasian, Cruikshank, Mayer, Pintrich, Raths, & Wittrock, 2001), some verbs that are commonly associated with those levels, and a few sample questions:

levels of Bloom's Revised Taxonomy	related verbs	sample questions
remembering	name, describe, list	Can you list the planets?
understanding	interpret, infer, summarize	What do you think an astronaut's day consists of?
applying	use, implement, execute	How much do you weigh on Venus?
analyzing	deconstruct, outline, organize	Outline some of the purposes of space exploration.
evaluating	check, critique, detect	Pluto has now been classified as a dwarf planet. Critique this decision.
creating	design, invent, plan	What missions would you prioritize next for NASA? What would your plan be for the next fifty years?

Want to extend this idea and make questions even more powerful in your classroom? Teach students to write questions for each level.

Methods of Engagement

Ask, "Whodunit?"

Everyone loves a good mystery. How about donning your deerstalker cap and getting your students involved in a whodunit as a strategy for creating an accessible and universally-appealing lesson?

Begin with a compelling mystery to be explored and/or solved:

› Where is Amelia Earhart?

› Who really invented the light bulb?

› What happened to the dinosaurs?

› Who killed President Garfield?

› What is my chance of winning the lottery?

› What started the Great Chicago Fire?

Then, gather primary (e.g., letters, photographs, newspaper articles, journal entries) and secondary (e.g., text book passages) sources that can serve as clues for students. Clues should inspire students to explore the presented question, make connections, and generate theories. For example, if students are given a clue about germs and infections and another about Garfield's long struggle to recover, they might begin to conclude that it was not a gunshot alone that killed the President.

Invite guesswork as students collaborate, engage in research, and discuss their findings.

Finally, create a forum for students to share their conclusions. You might wrap up by leading students in a whole-class discussion, by having them present to one another, or by bringing in a guest speaker to lecture on the mystery question.

Day 96

Question Them All

Seeking new ways to bring rich questions into the classroom? Try blanketing the room with them.

Write individual questions on index cards and give one to each student in the class. Provide them with time to formulate a response, or assign this task as homework. Then, throughout the week, call on individual students to read their question and answer aloud. Or, have students share their questions and answers with several different partners throughout the week.

Create different kinds of questions for different learners. Vary them by length, complexity, and type.

Day 97

Make A Circle

Inside-outside circle (Kagan, 1994) is a popular collaborative structure that provides learners with opportunities to connect with several classmates in a short period of time. It is a winner for the UDL classroom because it provides opportunities for socialization, lets students move, and has many uses (e.g., review, assessment).

To create an inside-outside circle, have half of the students in your class make a ring facing out; that is, they should be facing the four walls of the classroom. Then, direct the other half of the students to make a circle around that group; these students should be facing the students in the inside circle.

To begin this activity, give students a prompt to discuss, a problem to solve, or a question to explore with the partner they are facing. After a few minutes, ask them all to rotate. One circle should move clockwise one "notch" or person, and the other should move counterclockwise one "notch" or person. Repeat the prompt, problem, or question to give students multiple opportunities to explore the same material, or change the prompts with each rotation to provide the group with opportunities to discuss a range of issues.

Day
98

Fill In The Blanks

Have some party-style fill-in-the-blank fun in the classroom today by introducing a thought-provoking open-ended exercise. A fill-in-the-blank sheet can get students thinking and move them out of the habit of seeing just one correct answer for every question. Sentences should encourage students to think broadly and creatively.

Prompts for studying American government might include the following:

> The U.S. president should be more _____.

> The U.S. president should not be able to _____.

> The most important role of a vice-president is to _____.

> To put it in a nutshell, the secretary of state's job is to _____.

> One odd thing about U.S. elections is _____.

> U.S. senators should be required to _____ before taking office.

Once students finish, you can have them discuss their answers in small groups. Groups can then combine their answers or vote on the best responses to each item. Finally, have students share their ideas in a whole-group setting or submit them as assignments or exit tickets.

Day 99

Integrate Interests

Many students with disabilities—especially those on the autism spectrum—have deep interest in one or a variety of topics. Tap into these passions, interests, and gifts in order to create lessons, supports, and adaptations. Have a student who loves washing machines? Use a washing machine user guide to teach reading. Develop math problems involving laundry terms (e.g., "If one rinse cycle is 15 minutes and you cut it short by six minutes, how long did you rinse your shirts?"). Teach vocabulary related to laundry (e.g., agitate). Encourage some independent study about "how things work." Have the student write a critique or review of a favorite washing machine.

Day 100

Choose Choices

Every day and throughout the year, all students should be given choices about the type of work they do, their activities, and the ways in which they spend their time. Choice gives students a feeling of control in their lives and provides an opportunity for them to learn about themselves. Students themselves usually know when they are most creative, productive, and energetic; what materials and supports they need; and in what ways they can best express what they have learned.

Choice can be integrated into almost any activity. Give your fourth graders a choice of five different ways to practice their multiplication tables. Let your high school biology classes choose some of the labs they will conduct. Allow your preschoolers to select where they want to sit during work time (e.g., in the loft, at a table).

Other choices that might be given include

> work alone or with a peer;

> conduct your research in the library or stay in the room and work;

> type on your laptop or write in your notebook;

> use a calculator, count on your fingers, use manipulatives, or solve the problems in your head;

> choose any topic for your research paper;

> start your homework or find an educational game to play; and

> complete half of the problems on the page.

Say Cheese

If a picture is worth a thousand words, why not use one to get your students writing? Simply provide an interesting snapshot and ask students to respond to it in any style, format, or genre they choose. Invite the creation of comic strips, articles, essays, short stories, graphic novels, and even short screenplays.

This type of lesson gives students choices and allows them to show off their strengths and preferred writing styles.

Have students submit images for this exercise or grab them off one of these picture-rich sites:

> www.thewriteprompts.com

> www.visualwritingprompts.wordpress.com

> www.visualprompts.weebly.com

Methods of
Action & Expression

Send Them To The Corner

Multiple choice doesn't have to be dull. Get students moving today by making your classroom into a multiple-choice game board.

Simply assign a letter to each corner of your room so that you have corners A, B, C, and D. Call out a question and four possible answers. Then, ask students to move to the corner that corresponds with their chosen answer.

You can call out the correct answers as you go, or you can ask several questions in a row and share the answers at the end of the exercise.

To make this game a bit more challenging and a little more interesting, ask students to submit their own questions. Encourage them to think creatively and to focus on the most important learnings of the target lesson or unit, rather than on extraneous details.

Day 103

Get The Gist

When you have a few extra minutes left in a lesson, use it to let students consider the most critical pieces of content they learned that day, that week, or during an entire unit.

Simply instruct students to write the main idea at the top of a page; this is the gist. Then, have them add three details about that topic; this is the list. For this part of the exercise, be sure to encourage students to peruse their notes and their textbooks so they can mine for facts, illustrations, and potentially overlooked or already forgotten ideas.

If time permits, have students repeat the exercise with a partner.

 **Try Top 5s**

Top 5 lists are a no-fuss formative assessment strategy as well as a method for creating useful classroom visual supports. Lists can be used to review a unit or lesson, or to inspire new questions or extensions of learning.

To use this strategy, put students into small groups and ask them to brainstorm the "Top 5" things they have learned during a given day, week, unit, or lesson. Have them create their lists using colorful markers and chart paper. If some students struggle to write, you can provide groups with sentence strips, stickers, and sticky notes with pre-written messages on them.

Then, have each group present their list to the class or to another group. As groups share their work, ask follow-up questions or prompt them to add phrases, words, or images to make their lists more detailed, comprehensible, and clear.

Finally, post your lists in the classroom as a learning tool. Encourage students to add to them as they continue to learn. Sticky notes can be used as addendums to the original lists.

Wander To The Whiteboard

Want to hear from all of the students in your classroom? Try this simple processing exercise. Give markers to a few students, and ask them to write or draw something related to a topic or question on the whiteboard (e.g., "What is mythology?"; "Show me different ways to represent one half").

Once the first students have written something, have them pass their markers to others who have not yet shared. Repeat this process until everyone has shared, or continue one or two rounds to let students make connections between ideas and add to their original contributions. Then, examine the board as a class and use the words, fragments, sentences, and images as discussion points or writing prompts.

This exercise lets students learn from one another and provides an opportunity to hear every "voice" in the classroom.

Day 106

Debate It

There is just no arguing that debate is a win-win for the UDL classroom. This dynamic lesson format motivates students to dive into complex material, and provides opportunities to polish a wide range of skills including framing an argument, using vocal variety, and providing cogent responses to questions. With its emphasis on critical thinking, research, and teamwork, debate teaches skills that serve students well across grade levels and even beyond the school years.

In a debate, students can be given roles based on their strengths or their needs. Some might be assigned roles as researchers, while others shape the arguments. Still others may want to develop a visual outline of the points that will be emphasized.

To use debate, follow these simple steps:

> Assign students to a team.

> Give them a position to defend.

> Provide them with research materials.

> Give them time to gather information and discuss their findings.

> Ask them to present arguments in support of their position.

Teach about the content, but also about the process as students learn to use this structure. For instance, remind them to address the group and not just the instructor, and to speak only when it is their turn to do so.

For more on using debate in the classroom, visit www.idebate.org.

Vary Your Prep

Test prep is an inevitable part of teaching today. As you prepare learners for their standardized tests, and even for their curriculum-based assessments, use a variety of techniques so that you reach them all.

Some students will pick up skills and information from practice tests. Others may profit from learning stress-reduction strategies. Still others may want to work with peers to create and solve their own test-prep problems.

As you make decisions and implement strategies, be sure to talk to students about them. Help students evaluate methods with you, when possible. Ask them to identify which prep strategies worked and which ones did not.

Draw, Show, Or Tell

Provide your students with regular opportunities to show understanding in three different ways.

Share a question or prompt and tell students they may write or draw their answer, provide it verbally, or respond via a short demonstration. After students have designed or practiced their initial responses, have them get into triads. In these groups, they should ideally have all three types of responses represented—drawing, showing, and telling. If several students choose the same method, some triads may have only two types of answers represented.

Give learners some time to present to one another. After they finish presenting, have them compare and contrast the different ways they understood and illustrated the material.

Encourage students to try all three types of responses throughout the year.

Day
109

Act Out Aesop

If you are uncertain about a student's comprehension of content, be sure to provide him or her with many ways to demonstrate understanding.

Some students struggle mightily with comprehension questions, but can demonstrate understanding by engaging in a retelling or illustrating significant events in the book, chapter, or story. Students may also be able to show what they know by

> having a conversation with their peers/teacher,

> writing a short reflection,

> circling key words/pictures,

> create a Reader's Theater script,

> commenting in a small group discussion,

> filling in a story web,

> acting out the material, or

> assembling images related to the content.

Assemble A Panel

In a UDL classroom, it's always helpful to have a range of alternatives to presentations or reports. Panel discussions are a perfect replacement for more traditional structures, as they allow every student to participate and to demonstrate academic, communication, and literacy skills.

To use panels, put students into groups and assign each one a topic to research. Then, provide time for the group to study the topic and give a short presentation. Finally, open up the floor to questions from the class.

To create the best possible experience for students, be sure that every group has an understanding of the topic before they present to the class. You will also want to be sure that they have an understanding of what it means to serve on a panel. So, consider showing learners some footage of panel discussions à la *Meet the Press*.

Don't forget about the rest of the class! Give them some tips on how audiences typically interact with panels (e.g., questions are asked one at a time, audience members need to be recognized by a moderator in order to speak). You can also assign varied roles to your audience members to make the experience richer and to keep them engaged. So, if your panel consists of experts on alcohol and its effects on young people, you might have students in the audience play the role of concerned parents, teenagers, teachers, or doctors.

Be A Gamer

Today, have your students spin, roll, draw, quiz, or strategize their way into learning.

Put them into pairs or small groups and ask them to create a board game that will teach players about the curriculum. Students will surely be excited about this task and may even surprise you by using their creations outside of the classroom, which extends their learning beyond the confines of a particular unit.

Ask students to follow some simple rules as they construct their games. For example, you could ask them to

> relate the game to a lesson or unit (e.g., *Fraction Fun* or *Do You Know Newton's Laws?*),

> help the players learn or practice a skill and/or remember content,

> create simple rules that students in the classroom can easily read/follow, and

> design the game so that students can finish playing at least once during a class period.

Allow Retakes

Do your students all seem to learn at different paces? In most classrooms, the answer is an unequivocal "yes." One way to deal with this diversity is to allow students to take tests more than once. While this might seem unconventional, it is actually a common-sense approach to meeting the needs of all. If the purpose of UDL is to honor differences and provide avenues to learning success, then retesting students will likely increase student mastery of required content.

If you adopt this policy, be sure to talk to students about their responsibilities when it comes to retesting. Teach them how analyze their errors and challenges. Encourage them to develop study plans. Ask them to set a goal for the test (e.g., to achieve a 90% or better on the retest).

Methods of Action & Expression

Review & Repeat

During classroom discussions, many students hear little of what their classmates have to say. Instead, they focus primarily on what the teacher is sharing and look to him or her as the centerpiece of the conversation. To disrupt that pattern and promote active listening, start asking students to summarize the responses of their peers.

Having students summarize or repeat the contributions of others fosters active participation and promotes the idea that learning is a collaborative enterprise. In addition, most students will listen more attentively if they think they might be called upon to summarize a classmate's response.

Mic It Up

Celebrate your writers, performers, and orators by scheduling regular open mic time. Invite students to stand up and read their work, give an argument, or perform a piece for the rest of the class. This practice communicates to students that writing can be tied into performance, and that it can be used to connect with others. For some students, open mic will serve as an opportunity to use complete sentences. For others, it will be a chance to improve on speaking in a clear and confident voice. For still others, it is a chance to work on skills related to nonverbal expression.

Progress With Portfolios

Have you used portfolios in your classroom? If not, you might consider experimenting with them this year, as they are rich with opportunities for reflection and assessment.

Portfolios are a purposeful selection of work samples, artifacts, and other evidence of learning. The collection represents the student's goals, abilities, and progress and is used to evaluate a student's growth over time. The best part of portfolios is that each one can be as unique as the student who is assembling it.

Products that might be included in a portfolio include

> journal entries;

> writing samples;

> pieces of art;

> photographs;

> projects;

> tests, quizzes, and rubrics;

> maps, charts, graphs, and diagrams;

> checklists, anecdotal records, and lists;

> reading logs;

> interactive notebooks;

> Foldables™;

> self, peer, and teacher reflections; and

> family responses.

Portfolios are a useful assessment approach for students with a range of needs because they allow teachers to honor all kinds of abilities, including those not commonly assessed with other tools such as critical thinking, problem solving, leadership, creativity, and collaboration. Further, many different skills and competencies can be evaluated in a portfolio so teachers can use them to assess standards-based content, personal learning targets, and IEP objectives all at once.

Encourage Independence

One of the challenges for teachers in the UDL classroom is helping students with unique learning profiles succeed during segments of independent work. Some students struggle to stay with a task for an extended period of time. Others cannot write or type easily or well. Still others need support to follow multi-step directions.

It will be important for any teacher to have a range of ideas to use in these situations. You can:

> Offer written work options (e.g. laptop, dry erase boards, pencil/paper).

> Scan worksheets and tests into tablets and use applications like PaperPort Note [Nuance Communications] or SnapType [SnapType] to let students complete tasks by typing.

> Set a timer and let students know how long they need to work.

> Use a step-by-step checklist to keep students on task.

> Check in at regular intervals with those needing more support.

Day 117

Roll 'Em

Shake up the learning reflection after your next lesson by using this simple tabletop game.

Begin by putting students in small groups and giving each a die. Then, have each student in the group roll a number and answer a question based on that number. Use these prompts or create your own:

> 1 = One thing I learned today was . . .

> 2 = The main idea from this lesson was . . .

> 3 = Something I already knew was . . .

> 4 = A song that reminds me of today's lesson is . . .

> 5 = A word that represents today's lesson is . . .

> 6 = An image that represents today's lesson is . . .

Be aware that some students may need a little support to successfully answer your prompts or questions, so consider offering those learners a "cheat sheet" of cues or sample answers. You can also modify this game by changing the materials; instead of using a die from a game board, shop around for larger plush or foam dice that will be easier for students with motor problems to manipulate.

Reverse The Review

In a traditional classroom review session, students fire questions at the teacher and passively listen for answers they may need for an upcoming assessment. In this process, learners spend most of the review seeking the correct answers and very little time discussing, exploring, and thinking about their questions.

Why not try a reversal of this process in order to encourage your students to consider multiple or more complex answers to their questions?

In a reverse review session, the instructor poses questions and the students tackle them individually or in small groups. You can provide all of the questions at once and give a set amount of time for students to hunt for answers, or you can ask the questions one at a time, allow learners a few minutes to develop responses, and discuss each item as a class.

Write Without A Pencil

Many students either cannot write with a pencil, struggle to do so, or are simply more creative and expressive when given opportunities to compose in other ways. To give these students opportunities to express themselves, introduce websites that give them different ways to share their ideas.

Try for instance:

› www.magneticpoetry.com: This site lets users arrange word and phrase "fridge magnets" by dropping, dragging, and assembling them on their computer screen. Young learners can work on creating simple sentences, while older students can create questions, lists, or content-related metaphors.

› www.redkid.net: Click over to their Mad Libs section. Topics range from Little Red Riding Hood to Benjamin Franklin, and students need only to be able to type single words or phrases to compose an entire story.

› www.storybird.com: If you have not yet tapped into this gorgeous site, you will want to explore it as a teacher or as a writer yourself. Storybird allows users to create beautiful picture books. Students can browse thousands of illustrations, and drag and drop their favorites onto the pages of their e-book. They can then type a few words, add sentences or paragraphs, or creatively assemble the images to tell a story without words.

Make Your Case

Put your students "on the case" today by introducing a method of teaching that is engaging and teaches real-world skills and competencies.

In the case-teaching method, students review a real-world situation or "case" that poses a dilemma of sorts. Students are placed in the role of decision maker and asked to solve a problem. They have to sort out and analyze information presented, draw conclusions, and present solutions. Through whole-class discussion, small-group work, and potentially through multiple readings of related documents, learners have opportunities to immerse themselves in content.

To use case method in the classroom, follow these steps:

> Introduce the case.

> Give students ample time to read, explore, and think about the case.

> Create groups and direct them to design solutions to the problem.

> Have groups present their solutions.

> Ask clarifying questions and comment on contributions.

> Summarize the case and the process.

The case-teaching method is a good choice for the UDL classroom because you can use such a wide variety of methods to engage learners. Students can discuss ideas and present their views using discussion groups, debate, role-play, visuals, voting, and message boards.

Day
121

Cover Up

This alternative to a whole-class Q & A session involves having students work in small groups to generate as many ideas as possible in a short period of time. Start by distributing several sticky notes to each student and posing a question to the group. For example, "In five minutes, write down as many words as you can with the Latin root *co*," or "In one minute, write down what you already know about D-Day."

Each student then writes down as many answers as they can think of—one idea per sticky note—and affixes them to their table or shared desk space. Each group should generate as many ideas as possible and paper their desks or tables with the notes.

The responses can serve an informal assessment. They can also be used to start small-group or whole-class discussions.

Methods of Action & Expression

Make A List

Lists are a fun alternative to quizzes, tests, and other structured assessments. They are sure to delight our more linear learners, and their open-ended nature can appeal to creative types as well. Use lists to take a pulse on learning (e.g., "List five things you have learned so far in this unit"), to introduce a new topic (e.g., "List everything you already know about the Supreme Court"), or to spark curiosity and conversation (e.g., "List three ways that science can be dangerous").

To make this process as accessible as possible, be sure to offer a choice of tools to your list makers. Let them work with computers, tablets, pencils or markers, or even sidewalk chalk and a section of the playground.

Show It If You Know It

In a universally-designed classroom, it is critical that students have a variety of ways to show what they know. This is important not only to keep instruction lively and interesting, but also to support students who cannot easily express what they know.

Students can "show it if they know it" by

> demonstrating/performing a task;

> role playing/acting out a response;

> circling a response;

> using manipulatives;

> designing a chart, diagram, or map;

> choosing or taking a photo;

> making a poster or collage;

> creating a drawing or other piece of art;

> pointing to a card or object;

> pointing to a response on a communication board/choice board/app;

> indicating/responding on an interactive white board;

> holding up a response card (e.g., true/false); or

> providing a physical response (e.g., "Walk to the front of the room if you think the answer is_____, and to the back of the room if you think the answer is _____").

Today, consider using a new "show it" strategy in your classroom. Pick one idea from this list. Tomorrow, try another.

Methods of Action & Expression

Exhibit

If you are looking for a way to move beyond classroom presentations, consider implementing exhibitions this year. This strategy, popularized by Ted Sizer (Goldberg, 1993) and The Coalition of Essential Schools, is meant to provide rich, in-depth exploration of key concepts.

Exhibits consist of students presenting work to an authentic audience, sharing findings, and celebrating what they have learned. They can be used to conclude a long unit of study, or as a graduation requirement.

Exhibits often include oral presentations, but may also involve formal projects or portfolios. All of these experiences typically center on what the Coalition of Essential Schools calls "essential questions" (e.g., "What is culture?"; "Are we more connected than our ancestors were?"; "What are the unanswered questions of the oceans?"). These questions ask students to explore answers and to create new questions. That is, the exhibition is meant to engage the student in an intellectual investigation, not evaluate recall, memorization, or the regurgitation of the right answers.

Exhibits are authentic assessments that work well in the UDL classroom because they allow students to use a wide range of methods, incorporate their own interests, work independently or with partners, and access technology and other supports. Further, the exhibits allow educators to focus on different objectives for each individual learner.

Take Tickets

One of the easiest formative assessments to implement in your busy classroom is the exit ticket. Exit tickets are index cards or slips of paper that students hand to you, deposit in a box, or post on the wall as they leave your classroom. On the ticket, students respond to a question, solve a problem, or summarize their understanding of a concept or idea that has just been studied or presented.

To use tickets as a UDL tool, take some time to read the responses and use them to inform your instruction.

You can use exit tickets to

> group students for subsequent lessons (e.g., those who understand the lesson/those needing more support/those struggling with the content),

> pair students with a partner for a follow-up activity (e.g., "Today, I am pairing you with someone who had a similar exit ticket response to your own. Working together, combine your responses into one answer, blending ideas from both and providing an even more detailed response to the question."),

> take a pulse of the class as a whole (e.g., Have most of them mastered double-digit addition?; Do they seem to have a clear understanding of what symbolism is?), or

> prompt discussion in a subsequent lesson (e.g., "Most of you feel that Pasteur acted unethically in his experiments and that the ends did not justify the means. A few of you disagreed. Would Jen, Robin, or Shu-Li like to share why they disagree?").

Do Your Research

Research papers are a staple in both elementary and secondary schools; therefore, all teachers need ideas for assigning them. Consider the following ideas for making this common assignment accessible and appropriately challenging for all:

> Provide explicit step-by-step directions in a checklist format (with pictures if needed).

> Provide several examples.

> Provide templates or graphic organizers for steps of the process.

> Offer choices in format (e.g., develop a presentation or complete a project).

> Let students select their own topics.

> Provide links to websites with tips for citing sources, managing time, and organizing materials.

> Let students submit multiple small papers or one longer paper.

> Assign intermediate due dates (e.g., topic selection, first draft) so that students are assessed and get feedback before they complete their papers.

> Make sure students know where and when they can get help if they need it.

Day 127

Expand The Offerings

Assessments should help us determine what students need. To get the best information, however, we need to employ multiple measures, tools, and strategies across the week, month, and school year. All teachers know students who struggle on traditional assessments, but "show up" very differently when working on projects, engaging in a discussion, or creating a model.

Begin by doing a quick survey of your plans to get an idea of how many different tools you are already using. Then, review books, websites, and blogs to get ideas for new assessments you would like to try.

Need ideas? Consider trying one of these assessment tools in your next lesson. In fact, to make this recommendation more meaningful, put a (*) by one or two ideas you have not tried, but might want to try; a (+) by one or two ideas you would just like to learn more about; and a (#) by one or two ideas that you used in the past, have not used lately, and would like to try again:

> Annotated bibliography
> Art exhibit
> Blog post
> Bulletin board
> Case study
> Data analysis

> Focus group
> Learning station
> Literary analysis
> Magazine
> Musical performance
> Newscast

> Newspaper
> Photo essay
> Podcast
> Poster session proposal
> Student interview
> Survey

Day 128

Study Up

You may not be there when your students are preparing for your class, but that doesn't mean that you cannot help them improve their study skills. Take time to regularly teach students how to study and, further, how to differentiate when they do. That is, you will want to remind them to use a range of strategies and to continually assess and refine their methods so that they implement the ones that are most appropriate to their learning style and needs.

Study strategies you may want to teach include

> using flashcards or flashcard apps,

> reviewing notes (e.g., going over content with highlighters, adding icons/images, adding details),

> overlearning/repetition,

> engaging in peer Q & A,

> participating in study groups,

> podcast listening/video clip viewing,

> taking practice tests, and

> paraphrasing and rewriting content.

Study habits you can introduce include

> exercising or taking a short walk before a study session,

> maintaining an orderly and well stocked work area,

> studying in the same place/at the same time each day,

> keeping an organized notebook/planner, and

> taking breaks.

Sing

Teachers in UDL classrooms are constantly seeking new ways to teach, support, and inspire. Using music is one way to do all of those things within one lesson.

You can use music in many different ways, but perhaps the easiest application is to have students create a jingle, song, or rap about the content you are teaching. Put them into small groups and assign each one a standard or learning target. Then, provide guidelines for writing and performing. For instance, you may want to require that a certain phrase is repeated a number of times.

After giving the groups time to write, refine, and rehearse, let each one sing for the class. You might even want to provide a box of musical instruments (e.g., bells, rhythm sticks) and costume accessories (e.g., scarves, feather boas) in case some groups want to "punch up" their performances with props.

Want to make the learning last? Audio record or video record the performances. Then, play them during transition times, post them on your classroom blog, or insert them into lectures.

Day 130

Make A Meme

Collaborate with Ryan Gosling, Willie Wonka, or a basket of cute kittens in your next lesson by asking students to study and create internet memes.

A meme typically consists of a word or phrase that is cleverly paired with an illustration or photo and passed around the internet via social networking. Like cartoons, tables, pictograms, diagrams, and infographics, memes communicate a lot using few words. This makes designing them a "picture perfect" activity for UDL classrooms, where multiple literacies are valued.

You don't need a lot of time to engage students in the creation of a meme. Most of them have undoubtedly seen countless examples of this art form, so they will likely find the task both fun and familiar.

Another attractive element of this assignment is how accessible it is for students with unique learning profiles. Students can participate by simply choosing or taking a photo, adding a few words, and connecting it to the lesson. Those needing more challenge can be asked to play on metaphors, to engage in social commentary, or to create thoughtful calls to action.

Day 131

Doodle Away

In years past, students caught doodling may have been reprimanded or even punished. At the very least, they were likely told to "stop drawing and pay attention." Well, that was then and this is now. Today, a growing body of research (Ainsworth, Prain & Tytler, 2011; Andrade, 2010) suggests that doodling can actually help learners retain what they hear. Therefore, allowing students to doodle may not only help them "stay put" during long periods of inactivity, but also improve their comprehension.

So go ahead. Have students draw those sound waves. Encourage them to create a cartoon of The Battles of Lexington and Concord. Invite them to sketch "symmetry" in three different ways. You may even want to teach the art of doodling to one, more, or all students.

Be Comical

Kids love comics, right? So why not have your students create their own strips illustrating what they have learned in a particular unit or lesson? While they have certainly all been consumers of comics, it is likely that only a few of your students have had extensive experience working with this unique art form.

Creating comics allows students to demonstrate knowledge in a variety of ways. Strips can be used for note taking, a comprehension check, or a formal or informal learning assessment. They can also be assigned to encourage reluctant writers; students who resist producing free verse, a journal entry, or an autobiography might be quite willing to do so when they can complete the assignment with pen, ink, and a comic book template.

Students can also use software, apps, or websites to create their products. Sites you may want to bookmark for this purpose include the following:

> www.makebeliefscomix.com

> www.toondoo.com

> www.wittycomics.com

> www.marvel.com/games/play/34/create_your_own_comic

Before your students start creating, be sure to share plenty of comic strip examples. And consider providing a mini-lesson or two on drawing characters, writing dialogue, and storyboarding.

Day 133

Take A Minute

Today, try an exercise that will allow students to respond to a prompt in their own way and at their own level. After a lesson or mini-lecture, give them one minute to write an essay. Here are some sample prompts:

> - What is exercise?
> - Describe surrealism.
> - Why do hot things (hot air) rise above cold things (cold air)?

> - What are some of the effects of smoking on the body?
> - What are some of the differences between life today and life in the 1900s in our area?

You can also get creative with the one-minute paper. Try these unexpected options:

> - Hollywood is making a movie of Nat Turner's Rebellion/the life of Jonas Salk/*The House on Mango Street*. Cast the major characters and explain your choices.
> - List as many uses for a pencil/magnet/college degree as you can.
> - Create a soundtrack for gravity/a filibuster/CPR. Explain why you chose each song.

> - Design a metaphor for linear equations/Watergate/the skeletal system.
> - Share a few Twitter-style posts from Julio César Chávez/oxygen/an improper fraction.

Another good use of this strategy is to ask questions such as, "What was the main point of today's class?" or "What is one new word/term/idea you learned today?" These questions provide a general assessment of understanding and can serve as a tool for planning new learning experiences.

Listen To Your Writers

Every teacher has had a student who resisted putting pencil to paper or fingers to keyboard. Reluctant writers may need any number of supports, but one that is almost always needed is inspiration. One idea for launching a less-than-enthusiastic writer is to get him or her talking; that is, use speech as a springboard.

If you hear a student recite scenes from movies, copy the dialogue onto paper and cue her to use it as a story starter. If a young writer in your classroom shares a joke, encourage him to turn it into a post for the classroom blog. If the music teacher tells you that one of your students writes rap songs, ask her to turn those songs into poems.

Day 135

Catch It

This quick review game can be used as an energizer, or it can be extended and used as a whole-class discussion starter. It is useful not only for review purposes, but also for teaching new communication skills, as it provides opportunities for students to paraphrase, listen, and build on ideas that others have shared.

You will need a ball that can easily be tossed around the room for this exercise. To begin, hold the ball and generate a question that can be answered on many different levels, such as, "Why read fiction?" or "What is America's role in the world?" Then, throw the ball to a student who has an answer to the question. After he or she shares their response, comment on it, clarify any misconceptions, and, if necessary, ask a follow-up question or two.

Then have the student throw the ball to another student who wants to contribute. Before the second student answers, however, have him or her repeat what the previous student shared. Continue the process, with every student reviewing the previous answer before sharing a new response.

Go For A Goal

As teachers, we spend a lot of time setting goals for students. How much time, however, do we spend letting students set some of their own goals? How many books do students want to read? What grades do they want? What after-school activities do they want to pursue? What score do they want on the test? What skills do they want to acquire? All of these questions are appropriate for students to answer, potentially set goals around, and assess throughout the year.

To use goal setting in the classroom, share some of your own goals. Be sure to provide examples that are measurable and observable; in other words, it should be clear to everyone (a) what the goal is/looks like and (b) what must happen for the goal to be achieved. Then, provide examples of goals that students may want to set for themselves. Again, be sure that the goals you outline are both observable and memorable. For instance, a goal of "doing better on math quizzes" is vague, but a goal of "getting a B or better on every quiz until the end of the year" is both observable and measurable.

After they have crafted their own goals, have students talk to one another about plans for implementation. Ask them to consider how they plan to address their goal/s, how they are going to deal with obstacles, and how they are going to assess their progress.

To get students more involved in goal setting, you might

› let them create goals for different areas of their lives (e.g., learning, behavior),

› encourage them to share their goals with each other,

› provide time for creating goal-setting products (e.g., checklists, goal "reminder cards"), and

› set aside time to celebrate goals that have been reached.

Use AAC For All

If some of your students use augmentative and alternative communication (AAC), why not ask all students to use it at some point? Give everyone the option to either speak or write a response during a group sharing activity. Incorporate a few American Sign Language words into your lessons. Have all students hold up communication cards instead of shouting out answers. Let learners occasionally dialogue on paper with a partner in lieu of participating in group discussions.

This strategy will not only give AAC users opportunities to communicate effectively in a broader range of situations, but will also provide them with communication models as they learn new systems, tools, and devices.

Day 138

Land The Interview

Interviews give students a unique way to show what they know while providing the teacher with a flexible and sometimes eye-opening tool for collecting data. Students sometimes "show up" in conversations very differently than they do on paper, so this tool helps educators learn about the interviewees themselves while learning is evaluated.

To use interviews in the classroom, decide in advance what you want to know about students' knowledge and skills. Then draft a short list of questions and collect any manipulatives, props, or visuals that might be needed. For example, if you are teaching about weather, you might want students to identify weather instruments and show how they are used to take measurements.

Interviews can take place with individual students, while the rest of the class is engaged in independent work. You can also conduct interviews during daily lessons if you are co-teaching or if you have support from a paraprofessional during any segment of the day. If time is an issue (and it usually is), consider using focus group interviews instead of individual interviews. Focus groups often result in rich discussions that clarify misconceptions and lead to new learning. In fact, students participating in focus groups may walk away learning as much from the assessment as they did from the lessons that preceded it.

Day 139

Improvise

The world of improvisational comedy can be a great place to pick up new ideas for the universal design of lessons. Consider ideas that will allow students to think on their feet, have fun, be silly, and explore content in a new way.

Invite students to act out passages from the textbook (e.g., photosynthesis, Washington crossing the Delaware). Let them create humorous sketches about the ideas or concepts you study (e.g., You are an adverb and nobody in your family understands you; You are the endocrine system and you want to be a movie star). Assign groups to invent dances related to classroom content (e.g., Parallelogram Polka, Hydrogen Hop). Ask them to write and perform a funny dialogue for two people, ideas, or concepts you assign (e.g., an argument between Jefferson Davis and Gandhi).

Bust A Move

Movement is a key component of the responsive classroom. Build in time for students to move at regular intervals throughout the day so they feel alert, stay engaged, and retain what they are learning.

There are many ways to keep learners active in your classroom. You can try a "walk and talk" where you ask a question and have pairs of students wander around the classroom, playground, or even the school track for a few minutes before coming back to discuss their ideas with the whole group. You can try an alternative to hand raising by having students stand if they know the answer to a teacher's or fellow student's question. You might also integrate role-plays and short skits or use simulations, project-based instruction, and service learning to encourage interaction and engagement.

Day 141

Give The Thumbs Up

Keep students engaged in instruction by asking them to provide you with visual cues to indicate their level of comprehension. For instance, a "thumbs up" sign might indicate, "I understand." A sideways thumb might mean, "I'm getting it, but I still need a little more instruction." And a "thumbs down" sign might mean, "I am struggling with this material. I need help."

Other cues that can be used include

> sign language ("I understand"/"I'm lost"),

> colored cups (three cups stacked on the desk: green = "I understand"; yellow = "I'm getting it"; red = "I need help"), or

> dry erase boards (students write words/phrases to indicate level of understanding).

Use this information to sort students into groups, to plan follow-up activities, and to adjust your instruction on the spot.

Plan To Plan

Help your students succeed with studying, planning, and organizing. Some may need very little in terms of encouragement, strategies, and scaffolding, but others will need plenty. Be ready to provide different levels of support to different students. Some will only need to be provided with basic tools such as an assignment notebook, access to your blog, and a calendar app. Others may need a set time to review their assignments in the classroom and step-by-step guidance to create a system for managing materials. Still others may need peer or adult support to keep track of daily work and a detailed checklist for every single long-term project.

Act Like Socrates

Teach your students to speak like scholars by introducing them to the Socratic seminar. The Socratic seminar is a formal discussion, based on a text. In this structure, the teacher asks open-ended questions, and students are asked to think critically, share ideas, listen carefully, and respond thoughtfully to others' contributions.

Socratic seminars involve one learner talking at a time, and require students to work in a whole-class structure; therefore, some teachers may feel they are not a great fit for a UDL classroom. If attempts are not made to design seminars for students with a range of learning needs, this may be true. A few changes, however, can make this technique work well in every classroom.

To differentiate your Socratic seminars try one or more of these ideas:

> Co-teach a lesson, split the classroom into two groups, and use the strategy with much smaller groups of students, thus providing more potential talk time for every learner.

> Provide different roles for students. Some can present questions to the group alongside the teacher, and one or two can take visual notes during the discussion or serve as moderators.

> Give some or all students visual supports to boost their participation in the seminar. You might provide illustrated copies of participation rules, for instance.

> Show students short video clips of Socratic seminars so they can see and learn behaviors associated with the structure.

> Begin with texts that are short and easy to comprehend. As students become more skilled, you can introduce more complex selections.

Enter The Lesson

Today, add a little twist to a common formative assessment by moving exit tickets to the beginning of the class period.

"Entrance tickets" can be used in a variety of ways. As students enter the room, have them jot down what they learned from the previous day's lesson, share how they'd apply what they learned in a real-world scenario, or ask questions they may have about the upcoming lesson.

Use their responses to answer questions at the beginning of class, re-teach an important concept, or modify the day's lesson.

Want other ideas for "entering the lesson" with some feedback? Try these strategies:

> Ask a question such as, "What do you know about _____?"

> Have the group make predictions related to an upcoming lesson or learning experience.

> Ask students to "turn and talk" about a word, idea, concept, or image related to the day's lesson.

> Administer a survey about current knowledge of the day's topic.

> Assign a quick write.

Methods of Representation

Toss-A-Word

Looking for an activity to soak up some of those transition minutes after you finish a lesson and before students leave the classroom? Try a game of word wall ball. The only materials you will need are a toss toy and a classroom word wall.

Hand the ball to a student and ask him or her to throw it at the wall. When the learner hits a word, they need to define it or draw an example of it on the dry erase board.

There are many different variations of this game that you can try. For instance, you can have students throw the ball at

> a number line (students name numbers they hit or determine if the number is even or odd),

> a map (students name the state/region/country they hit),

> the periodic table (students provide information about the element they hit),

> the alphabet chart (students share words that begin with the letter they hit),

> a poster of warm-up exercises (students lead the class in the exercise they hit), or

> a name chart (students give a compliment to the person whose name they hit).

Visualize Visuals

If you are committed to reaching all learners, you will want to constantly consider the use of visuals in the classroom. Do you use enough visual supports? Are your visuals supporting student learning? Which visuals do you need for all students/some students/just a few students?

Visual aids can be used to provide interest and motivation; to increase retention of learning; to clarify a difficult, complicated, or abstract concept; or even to push students to think more creatively.

Try incorporating visuals such as:

> photos (e.g., examples of symmetry in nature),

> directions (e.g., pictures of the steps required to clean up cooking stations in a foods class; steps in peer editing),

> checklists (e.g., materials needed for a portfolio),

> anchor charts (e.g., Rules for Capitalization; How Do I Observe?), and

> infographics (e.g., Facts About Teen Suicide; Comparisons of World War I & World War II).

Get Organized

No matter what grade level or subject area you teach, it is likely you use graphic organizers in your classroom.

Graphic organizers are an incredibly flexible tool; they can be used to help students make sense of new information, activate prior knowledge, prepare to write or read, learn and dissect vocabulary words, outline concepts related to the text, and more.

Different organizers can be used for different learners; alternatively, you can use the same organizer for all, but scaffold it for those needing more complexity or more support. For instance, you may give some students a blank Venn diagram, and others a diagram with some content and all three titles already added.

See these links for free downloadable graphic organizers:

› www.studenthandouts.com

› www.freeology.com

› www.teacherprintables.net

And browse this table of graphic representation methods to get new ideas for teaching and learning:

› www.visual-literacy.org/periodic_table/periodic_table.html

Make It Tactile

Students who are blind, have low vision, or who just learn best when lessons are "hands on", often benefit from the use of tactile graphics (e.g., raised letter tiles, interactive picture books) and physical models (e.g., human skeleton, 3D shapes, salt and flour maps). You can either make these in advance or have students assemble them as part of a learning activity or assessment.

Fracture The Chapter

Make the exploration of textbook content easier and more interesting to your learners by fracturing your chapters.

Simply, divide the class into small groups and assign one section of the chapter to each group. Then, make each group responsible for reading their section, mining important points from it, and creating a short visual presentation to illustrate these points. They can use poster paper and markers or choose to use software such as PowerPoint, Keynote, or Prezi (www.prezi.com).

Then, give each group some time to share the critical elements from their section of the text. Be sure to designate sections of content based on the needs and abilities of learners. In some cases, you may even want to provide more complex text passages from other sources if a few learners in your classroom require more challenge than the assigned textbook provides.

 **Day 150**

Work With Words

Every educator needs to teach vocabulary all year long. To keep lessons interesting, use a wide range of techniques and provide opportunities for students to choose their learning methods when possible.

Tools you can use to teach and reinforce new vocabulary words include

> - acrostics;
> - computer games and apps;
> - drama games and skits;
> - word drawings;
> - personal dictionaries;
> - predictions;

> - word walls;
> - graphic organizers;
> - games like Jeopardy, Password, and Taboo;
> - word ladders; and
> - fill-in-the-blank sentences (e.g., I was incredulous because _____).

Choose one to two new ideas from this list to implement in your next lesson.

 Day 151

Know, Want & Learn

Many a teacher has used a KWL instructional reading strategy to guide students through a text. In most instances, this technique involves a class discussion and the completion of a three-column chart. The teacher typically scribes as students share what they know about a topic; this is listed in the "K" column of the chart. The group then generates a list of questions about what they want to know about the topic and those comments are placed in the "W" column of the chart. New information learned as the text is explored or after students finish reading is recorded in the "L" column.

This strategy can provide some helpful structure during a complex exploration of a text, but it can be a little challenging for some students. Try the following ideas for making your KWL more accessible for all:

> Participate in the KWL session. Add a comment or two in each section to get the ball rolling and to make sure that important ideas are included.

> Give some learners choices for parts of the exercise; not all students, for instance, could easily generate ideas for new learning, but most could point to or circle one thing they want to learn if given a few options.

> Make it a little more active. Have students move around the classroom until you give a cue (e.g., shut off the lights, ring a bell). When they see/hear the cue, they should immediately get into a group of two or three with those standing around them. This group can generate ideas for the first column. Then, repeat the process and have students get into a second group to brainstorm ideas for the second column. Repeat the process after students have read the selection/chapter/book and have them fill in the last column.

Tap Primary Sources

Make your lessons appealing for all by introducing a variety of primary sources. Teach with magazine articles, newspaper clippings, political cartoons, posters, and correspondence.

Primary sources are particularly valuable for universally-designed lessons because of their varied complexity, vocabulary, and forms. These materials also help students make a personal connection to content and tap into their natural curiosity about the world.

Further, the sheer variety of sources provides opportunities to create appropriate lessons for all. The same question or topic can be explored by all learners in the classroom, but those with more ability or knowledge in a certain area can be given more challenging assignments. For instance, some students might analyze a short postcard from a WWII soldier to his mother, while others explore a series of political cartoons satirizing Winston Churchill.

Students can also use the same materials and address different questions. You might have the entire class examine slave auction advertisements, but break the class into small groups to explore different aspects of the materials. Some may look for information about the practice of slavery itself, others may focus on what can be learned about the economics and business practices of the time, and still others may discuss content related to culture, norms, and beliefs.

Review In A Flash

Using flashcards is not a new idea in education, but a few tweaks can make it feel new. Students can absolutely go "old school" and study independently or with a partner, but there are many other ways to use this time-tested technique.

To incorporate flashcards into a lesson, distribute sets to individuals or small groups; have students decorate and personalize a set of these pre-made cards, or let them create their own sets using different kinds of media (e.g., markers, labels).

Then, incorporate the cards into lessons in any number of ways. You might, for instance, try these ideas:

> Show a flashcard and have students spend a minute sharing anything they know about the word, number, or concept.

> Show students a series of flashcards and ask them to write or repeat all of the cards they remember.

> Distribute one card to each student and have them teach their word/idea/fact to several different partners.

> Ask groups of learners to create a flashcard practice game or activity.

If you want students to take their session online, try these websites for flashcard review activities:

> www.cram.com

> www.quizlet.com

> www.studyblue.com

The best part of flashcards is that they can be customized for students or small groups. Different students can use different card sets, and different groups can practice skills using different games.

Highlight Patterns & Features

One way to support students in becoming powerful learners is to teach them how to decide what is critical and what is unimportant or irrelevant. The goal is for students to recognize key information, allocate their time efficiently, and identify what is valuable.

To help students with these skills, try:

> highlighting or emphasizing key elements in text, graphics, diagrams and formulas;

> using multiple examples and non-examples to emphasize critical features;

> using cues and prompts to draw attention to critical features;

> using outlines, graphic organizers, unit organizer routines, concept organizer routines, and concept mastery routines to emphasize important ideas and relationships; and

> highlighting skills that can be used to solve unfamiliar problems or tasks.

Slide Through Your Slides

Pecha Kucha is a presentation style where twenty slides are shown for twenty seconds each. Originating in Japan, this technique is typically used in the fields of design, architecture, photography, art, and academia.

You can bring this unique technique into your classroom as a way to support your visual learners. You can use it to teach lessons and let students use it to create their own presentations. Since the presentation—by definition—is short (about six minutes), most students find it more low-risk that a typical oral presentation, report, or demonstration.

This method works well in a UDL classroom, as content can vary. In other words, each student who creates a Pecha Kucha can have a different topic or focus. Additionally, students can easily bring in areas of interest. A student who is passionate about photography can take and use his own images. A learner who loves music can choose favorite songs to use as their Pecha Kucha soundtrack.

Check Your Output

As you are presenting, lecturing, or engaging in a whole-class discussion, be mindful of output. Do your students need more than spoken words to follow along and comprehend the material? Most will, so make sure to consider all the ways you "show and tell." You might have a PowerPoint or Keynote presentation as a support, or offer electronic notes that students can access online during or after the presentation. You could also introduce an app that gives learners opportunities to react to the material you are covering. Finally, you could integrate video to add variety to your presentation and enhance the lecture or discussion.

Highlight, Translate & Magnify

Most teachers use Microsoft Word daily. They use it to create lesson plans, related learning materials, forms, and assessment tools. Students also use Word on a regular basis. They use it to write, create artwork, and complete assignments. These are all appropriate uses. Microsoft Word, however, can do so much more. It has many features that can be used to teach new skills, adapt written materials, and support diverse learners as they work on-screen.

To create products that diverse learners can use, you can:

› highlight key words or phrases,

› add graphics,

› translate text into other languages,

› use borders so students can see where to attend or place an answer, and

› increase spacing between characters to make visual tracking easier.

If students are working on the computer, other tools might be employed. For instance, you can:

› adjust the background color of a document to increase visibility,

› enlarge the toolbar icons, or

› magnify the text on a student's monitor.

Students can also use Microsoft Word as a support for their own work. They can access:

› spelling and grammar check,

› the thesaurus,

› auto correct,

› the "track changes" feature, and

› outline templates.

Day 158

Say It

Students need to learn words in context. Vocabulary lessons alone won't do it. Decide on the words you want to teach your learners and integrate them into your daily conversations and lessons. Then, share them with your collaborative partners and encourage them to use these same words on a regular basis. Invite students to share examples of their *petulance* or their *altruism*. Ask them what they have an *affinity* for or what they *abhor*. When your day begins, remind them what time lunch will *commence*, and so on.

Compare & Contrast

Focus on comparisons to encourage students to dive deeper into lesson content. This practice will help students see similarities and differences between things and prompt higher-order thinking. Graphic organizers like comparison alleys and Venn diagrams work well for this. Instead of simply asking, "What is a civil war?" you can ask students to compare and contrast revolutions and civil wars. Instead of asking, "What is technology?" you can have them compare and contrast science and technology.

This task of organizing helps students focus on the connections between things they know and provides a foundation for them to explore what they do not know. It also allows them to participate in different ways. Some learners will be able to give more basic responses to comparison questions, while others will be able to elaborate, think in broader terms, and provide several examples.

Chalk It Up

Sidewalk chalk is inexpensive and well worth the dollar or two you will spend to include it in one or more lessons. Drawing and writing with chalk will be a welcome change for some of your students with motor problems, but it will likely be appreciated by all learners simply because it is different and gives them an opportunity to learn outside the classroom.

If you teach younger children, you can take your chalk to the blacktop. If you teach middle school or high school, you will need to find a patch of sidewalk or courtyard for your lesson.

Use the chalk to:

> Draw large-scale maps.

> Make beautiful works of art including mandalas, mazes, and murals.

> Create a hundreds chart, coordinate grid, or graph.

> Scrawl spelling words.

> Design a huge, multi-event chronology or time line complete with illustrations.

> Sketch the life cycle of a frog, the constellations, geometric shapes, simple machines, or the circulatory system.

> Write sidewalk poetry.

> Draw a life-size great white shark, dinosaur, Abe Lincoln, or Wright brothers' plane.

> Map out tenement housing apartments or The Oval Office.

If you like this idea, keep in mind you can "jazz things up" by introducing other materials like sidewalk paint, glitter chalk, and stencils.

Gather Materials Galore

Using a variety of instructional materials helps all students learn. Students who are studying United States geography and culture might be introduced to maps, globes of different sizes, brochures from different state landmarks, tour books, travel literature, new and "used" postcards, travel posters, vacation photos and videos from the families of students in the class, and apps and websites related to the U.S. and its people.

A selection of materials is important because it offers every learner a chance to be successful and learn in a way that suits them best. For instance, a student with low vision may be unable to effectively interact with an atlas or globe, but may be able to learn concepts easily by studying a salt and flour map of the country.

Show The Shark & The Sunflower

A picture can be used to inspire a discussion, build background knowledge, hook students on a new area of content, or encourage the development of questions. A picture of a breaching great white shark, a California migrant family in 1930, or a Fibonacci sunflower can get students talking, thinking, debating, and hypothesizing before a single piece of information is presented. At its most basic, this strategy can involve just showing the picture and asking for reactions. After the initial presentation of a Gettysburg field hospital, for instance, you can ask students to comment on what they see, or you can use guiding questions to encourage them to draw conclusions about the image.

You can also hand this task over to students. Each week you might assign a different student the task of selecting an image related to course content. Or you can get them involved in a more in-depth project such as the #mathphotoaday challenge started by a third-grade class on Twitter.

Using photos as a teaching tool is powerful because most visuals are accessible to most students. In addition, interpreting images is open-ended, and can be made more or less complex depending on the follow-up questions and comments provided by the teacher.

Look for pictures on the following sites:

> *The New York Times* (learning.blogs.nytimes.com/category/lesson-plans/whats-going-on-in-this-picture)
> *National Geographic* (photography.nationalgeographic.com/photography/photo-of-the-day)
> NASA (apod.nasa.gov/apod/astropix.html)
> *The Wall Street Journal* (blogs.wsj.com/photojournal/category/photos-of-the-week)

Translate, Teach & Support

Students learning English and those who are Deaf may need support to understand daily lessons and participate in classroom activities. For example, drama activities can be effective in reaching a wide range of students; acting out The Boston Tea Party might help those experiencing language barriers better understand that event.

Other ideas that may benefit these students include:

> using cooperative learning;

> giving clear visual and verbal directions;

> pairing students with language needs with learning partners who do not have the same language needs;

> teaching with concrete objects, models, visuals, and photographs;

> making key information available in both the dominant language and the students' first languages; and

> providing electronic translation tools or links to multilingual glossaries on the web.

Start A Silent Conversation

In a silent conversation, all of the steps of the process should take place without spoken words. It is an ideal activity for a multi-level classroom because it provides some support for students who are too anxious to participate in a traditional classroom discussion. It also provides an entry point for those who cannot produce a lot of text, as many different types of contributions are welcomed (e.g., doodles).

To begin, put students into small groups and give them a piece of text to read, an image to examine, or a film clip to view. After they have completed the task, prompt them to comment on what they have read, seen, or viewed by jotting questions and comments on a shared sheet of chart paper.

The written conversation must connect directly to the text, image, or clip, but can stray to wherever the students take it. If someone in the group writes a question on a related topic, for instance, another member of the group can address the question by adding a picture, word, or sentence, or by circling previously added comments.

As they complete the task, remind students that

› more than one of them can write on the page at the same time;

› both images and words can be added; and

› they can connect associated words/phrases and images with lines, circles, and other markings.

Sort It Out

A sure way to break out of a classroom rut is to introduce a game, and one of the easiest games to assemble is a card sort. To begin, consider the content you are teaching and create note cards related to concepts that can be classified, categorized, or ordered in two or more groups (e.g., examples of parts of speech, images related to various wars).

Put students in pairs. Hand out one set of materials to each group and ask students to sort them. You can begin by letting them sort the stack without sharing the target categories. This version of the game lets students explore materials and have discussions about all of their observations related to the content. They may come up with several ways to organize the deck at this stage. For instance, students might sort a stack of cards filled with names of U.S. cities into urban, suburban, and rural cities, and then into high-population and low-population cities. After this initial exploration, you could tell students what categories you want them to focus on for the final sort. If you want the city cards to be sorted into U.S. regions, provide learners with the name of each category (e.g., West, Midwest) or maybe even brightly colored category cards, so that each group has a visual support to use as they complete the task.

You can differentiate within this game by assigning learners different roles. One student may facilitate the sort, another may be responsible for fact checking, and a third may have the job of creating additional cards to add to the sort. You can differentiate further by giving out different sorts to different groups, with some sets being more challenging to complete than others.

Day 166

Get Close

Close readings are now common practice in classrooms, therefore, you will need strategies for designing this practice for a wide audience. Not all students will attack a reading in the same way, so be sure to have a range of ideas at hand. For instance, you might

> use re-readings (let students explore the text more than once),

> let students suggest readings to explore,

> provide accessible materials (e.g., enlarged text, e-readers) when needed,

> set the purpose for reading (write it down so students don't forget it),

> model behaviors associated with close reading (e.g., identifying evidence),

> introduce small pieces of text before longer passages,

> teach annotation,

> preview questions you will ask, or

> allow some or all students to work in pairs or in small groups.

Methods of Representation

Make A Metaphor

Charge students with creating metaphors and analogies to inspire creativity and to move into a deeper understanding of a concept. Metaphors and analogies help students tackle unfamiliar content by prompting them to make connections between something they know or understand and something that is new to them. Metaphors can also serve as motivators as comparisons can be linked to something students both know and like. For instance, you might ask students to consider how elections are like reality shows, how a cell is like *The Millennium Falcon*, or how jazz is like Facebook.

Day 168

Adopt An Ally

Learning Ally (www.learningally.org) is a national non-profit dedicated to helping those who are blind, visually impaired, and dyslexic. Started in the 1940s as Recording for the Blind, the organization utilized volunteers to record books for WWII veterans who returned home blind or with low vision. The site now offers the world's largest collection of human-narrated audio textbooks and literature, as well as solutions, support, and community for parents, teachers, and students.

Why audiobooks? Students can keep up on coursework even if they struggle with grade-level text, listen to fluent readers, and access a wide variety of titles without personal support.

Learning Ally is a great launch into the world of audiobooks for your students with disabilities. There are many titles to choose from and, since the books are read by people, they tend to be a bit more interesting than stories or textbooks accessed using a screen reader.

Think Big

Forget bulletin boards. If you want students to be dazzled, set to work on an epic visual that will turn heads and inspire innovation. How about creating a huge wall-sized periodic table, filled with images and objects that represent the elements? Or a long mural of the solar system that illustrates the relative distances between the planets? Or a massive map of the state in which you live? Or a chalkboard wall filled with poems students can create, change, and build collaboratively?

Draw, Guess & Learn

So many students learn best visually. To honor them, incorporate this game-show-esque drawing strategy into your mini-lectures and discussions.

Begin by choosing an illustrator. You can perform this function, or you can hand the responsibility to a student.

Select words related to classroom content and show them only to the illustrator. Then, have him or her draw (or attempt to draw) these words on chart paper or a dry erase board. Start with concepts that are fairly concrete and somewhat easy to draw and guess (e.g., valley, amphibian, acid, equation). When students are ready for a challenge, introduce concepts that are more abstract (e.g., calorie, independence, theory, Boyle's Law).

As the illustrator draws, have his or her classmates try to guess the image. Guesses can be shared until someone in the group identifies the picture.

If you want to get even more learners involved and bring the energy up a notch, consider inviting more than one illustrator to draw. You can have two or three students draw the same image for their own small groups. The game can then be a race to see which group guesses the correct answer first, or you can simply have groups work on the same words, but compete only within their own small circles.

Picture It

Picture books are great resources for students of all ages. Teachers in primary grades know this and use them across the curriculum to teach a number of skills, but educators in upper elementary grades, middle school, and high school may not understand the power of pictures to inspire, teach, and engage.

Picture books can be used as a supplement for class discussions and as a primary text for struggling readers. For instance, *A Million Fish . . . More or Less* by Patricia McKissack can be introduced during a lesson on statistics or graphs, *Pink and Say* by Patricia Polacco is a fantastic choice for teaching about the Civil War, *Those Darn Squirrels* by Adam Rubin can be integrated into a lesson on engineering design, and Paul Janeczko's *A Kick in the Head* can be read to teach poetic forms.

 **Day 172**

Toy With Them

Bring in props, toys, and unusual learning materials to emphasize points, elicit responses from students, and add humor to your daily lessons.

A classic choice is the rubber chicken. Buy them in bulk and use them not only as response objects but also as desktop fidget toys.

Magic wands are also a must. Get them at the dollar store and use them to motivate students to begin work; to tap a rhythm, syllables in a word, or numbers on a number line; to create 60-second fairy tales; or to simply sprinkle a little magic into an otherwise ho-hum lesson.

Don't forget to add a costume change or two. A feather boa can be passed from student to student to indicate whose turn it is to talk. It can be used in classroom skits. It can even be used as a funny form of nonstandard measurement. A ridiculous hat can be turned into a thinking cap. And a fabulous cape can transform a teacher or student into a superhero, capable of solving any problem or tackling any challenge.

Shrink It

Do you have useful visuals posted on your classroom walls to guide students as they work? If so, why not shrink these down and make portable copies for learners who may need them?

Some of your students may need desktop copies of

> maps,

> alphabet charts,

> number charts,

> tables,

> word walls,

> calendars,

> grammar/punctuation rules,

> multiplication/division strategies,

> diagrams,

> schedules,

> safety procedures, and

> work habit reminders.

You can laminate these shrunken visuals and attach them to students' desks. Alternatively, you can snap photos of them and load them on students' devices. You can even suggest that students choose a visual to use as a screen saver so they will have multiple opportunities to view and study it.

Revise The Textbook

One of the most common adaptations teachers make to a textbook is to change the content in some way. The material may need to be changed to better fit a learner's age, experiences, abilities, or reading level. Whole pages or chapters may be omitted or shortened for some of these learners. Other pieces of the text may simply be adapted. Teachers can adapt text in a number of ways. They can

> rewrite passages, sections, or chapters (to simplify the language or make it more complex);

> cut out or cross out certain passages, sections, or chapters;

> highlight or emphasize certain sentences or paragraphs;

> animate or create comic book versions of certain sections;

> supplement the text with easier or more challenging books or articles on the same topic; and

> summarize content into bulleted points.

In some cases, students can help the teacher with these adaptations. For example, they can personalize their own books with sticky notes, highlighter tape, and bookmarks or by accessing e-readers and the accessibility options available on them.

Frame Them

Many students have difficulty getting started and staying focused on an issue when asked to produce written responses. Writing frames can help these learners work more independently and learn how to organize their thoughts.

Writing frames consist of a skeleton outline. They help writers use appropriate text organization for summarizing information. For instance, frames may include sequence connectors (e.g., first, then, finally) that help students transition from one idea to the next.

So an essay on Martin Luther King Jr. might begin with the following sentences, phrases, and spaces:

> *Dr. Martin Luther King Jr. is famous for the contribution he made to the U.S. Civil Rights Movement. Dr. King was a _____*
>
> *who did many things to promote fairness, progress, and _____. He _____.*
>
> *He also _____. Finally, Dr. King helped promote fairness, progress, and _____*
>
> *by _____.*

Keep in mind that not all students will need writing frames and you can create more than one version if you have students needing more or less scaffolding than their peers.

Make Models

Many students love to create, design, and build. Let them do so by asking them to construct models.

Models can be made in any number of subject areas. For instance, students might recreate

> cells,
> body systems,
> land forms,
> animals or insects,
> the rock cycle,
> DNA,

> the ocean zones,
> an ecosystem,
> the Oregon Trail,
> a government,
> structures (e.g., Hoover Dam),

> natural disasters,
> ancient civilizations,
> the Space Shuttle,
> a plant or a leaf,
> a circuit,
> polyhedra,

> statistics concepts,
> a fraction,
> the atmosphere,
> landmarks,
> cities, or
> battles/battlefields.

This task encourages creativity, so students can draw on their strengths while they work. That is, the artists in the class can sculpt and paint, students who like to cook or bake can do so, and those who are into building can use Lego, blocks, or other materials to show what they know.

Want something grander than a tabletop model? Challenge students to transform your entire classroom into one big model. Have them craft a room-sized model of the human heart, the Taj Mahal, or the Atlantic Ocean.

Introduce Idioms

Some students struggle to understand aspects of English. Students learning the language certainly fall into this category, but many other learners including those on the autism spectrum, those with certain learning disabilities, and those who are Deaf and hard of hearing may also have needs in this area.

One aspect of English that is particularly challenging for many is figurative language. Understanding idioms, metaphors, irony, and hyperbole isn't easy. Therefore, even students without identified needs will profit from strategies that make this area of the language easier to comprehend. Try the following figurative language "busting" ideas:

> Teach figurative language across the curriculum.

> Explain expressions as you use them in the classroom.

> Provide opportunities to learn about language (e.g., teach a "metaphor of the week").

> Use visuals and picture books (e.g., *The King Who Rained*).

> Encourage students to keep "figurative language" dictionaries to learn and remember terms they hear.

Day 178

Assess & Activate Knowledge

Students who lack sufficient background knowledge may struggle to access, participate in, and progress through daily lessons. Therefore, it is critical that students' prior experiences are explored and any gaps in knowledge are addressed.

There are many ways to activate background knowledge. You can provide direct instruction on a topic; take field trips or virtual trips; use photographs, illustrations, and video clips; or conduct a class discussion. To be truly effective in building student background knowledge, however, you need to know where to begin; you must start by assessing what students already know.

To assess prior knowledge, you might use a group discussion, a journal prompt, or a KWL organizer. You might also use a prediction guide (Buehl, 2001). A predication guide provides clues about what's coming next and sets a purpose for learning. To create such a guide, provide students with a list of statements related to an upcoming unit of study. Then, have them indicate if they agree or disagree with each one. A prediction guide in a science class might ask students to respond to the following sentences:

> The sun is a star.
> Brighter stars are the closest.
> Stars are the largest bodies in the universe.

Direct students to do their best as they complete their guides, but be sure they understand that this activity is not a test, and that they will not be graded on their work. After the guides are completed, have a class discussion about the responses. Talk about misconceptions and how the statements connect to upcoming lessons. Then, collect the guides and use them to inform your planning.

Go To The Gallery

Let your students stroll, examine, appreciate, and learn today. To put it another way, host a classroom gallery walk!

To begin, have students create a visual representation of their learning (e.g., poster, 3-D model, graph) and post their creations around the room.

Then, invite the group to walk around and visit the various displays.

Provide guidelines for how students should interact with the pieces they are observing. You may want them to take notes on what they see or jot messages to the artist or creator on a tablet near each piece, for instance. You may also want to give them a goal for the activity such as viewing and examining at least 10 pieces in the classroom or asking at least three peers a question about their work.

Finally, add any flourishes that you think will set the appropriate tone. Play classical music. Serve carbonated water and healthy hors d'oeuvres. Invite guests to interact with students and comment on the posted works.

 **Day 180**

Break It Down

Break big tasks down into smaller parts for students who may feel overwhelmed by multi-step directions and large-scale projects. You may need to

> create step-by-step checklists,

> allow some or all students to hand in parts of their assignments as they are completed instead of waiting until all parts are completed,

> create a timeline for completing steps of a task (e.g., give a student reading a 200-page novel deadlines for finishing each chapter),

> put reminders to complete tasks on smartphones or tablets (or cue students to do this), and

> give examples of how you break larger tasks down in your own work or personal life.

Rinse & Repeat

Pick up one or two shower curtains at the dollar store and use them to "freshen up" a lesson or two. For younger students, curtains can be used as story maps as you can draw events from a book and have learners literally walk a retelling. You can also use them as oversized word walls that can be wiped clean when new words are added and old ones are mastered. Or, you can create a massive keyboard and let students slap out spelling words on the floor or wall.

For older students, this huge canvas can be used to create murals like those sponsored by the Federal Art Project, a timeline that can be marched across (e.g., the rise and fall of the Roman Empire), a game board filled with questions, or an interactive coordinate plane.

The best part about using a shower curtain in lessons is that it is reusable. You can have students use dry erase markers for these activities and wipe off their work when they finish.

Put Up A Poster

Students in your classroom understand the power of posters. Most of them likely have at least one in their bedroom that they selected for its message, meaning, or image.

Posters can serve as learning tools in two ways. You can use them to send students messages related to the work in a UDL classroom (e.g., "Fair does not mean equal. It means everyone gets what they need"). You can also use them as informal assessment tools. Ask students to play with backgrounds, text, photos, and composition to create products related to lessons. They may create posters to represent favorite quotes from a novel or powerful lines from a notable speech. These posters can fill a bulletin board or classroom wall.

Try these sites for printable posters perfect for the classroom:

> www.postermywall.com

> www.posteroven.com

> www.canva.com

Day 183

Try TED In The Classroom

Most teachers have used TED talks to bolster their own learning in some way, but these same educators may not be aware that this tool can be used with students. Many talks work well as supplements for discussions and lectures as they are short, to-the-point, and offered by some of the most respected researchers and ideologues in the world. Some of the talks frequently used with students include the following:

> *Why Believe in Others* by Victor Frankl
> www.ted.com/talks/viktor_frankl_youth_in_search_of_meaning

> *How I Built a Windmill* by William Kamkwamba
> www.ted.com/talks/william_kamkwamba_on_building_a_windmill

> *A Performance of "Mathemagic"* by Arthur Benjamin
> www.ted.com/talks/arthur_benjamin_does_mathemagic

> *Science is for Everyone, Kids Included* by Beau Lotto & Amy O'Toole
> www.ted.com/talks/beau_lotto_amy_o_toole_science_is_for_everyone_kids_included

> *A Teen Just Trying to Figure it Out* by Tavi Gevinson
> www.ted.com/talks/tavi_gevinson_a_teen_just_trying_to_figure_it_out

This list is, of course, only a sampling of what is available on www.ted.com. Visit often for material for your students and for ideas on how to present material creatively in your own classroom.

Map It Out

When students enter the classroom today, make markers, sticky notes, stencils, and poster paper available and invite them to create concept maps on their own, with a partner, or in small groups.

A concept map is a way of illustrating connections between terms or ideas. Students construct concept maps by connecting individual terms with lines that indicate the relationship between each set of terms. Most concept maps represent a hierarchical structure; the main concept is usually positioned at the top or in the middle, with sub-topics connected to that and branching off in all directions. Additional sub-topics, details, illustrations, and examples are drawn off of the first level of sub-topics and in between various bubbles, pictures, words, and phrases.

You can challenge some students to add extra details, to extend learning beyond concepts covered in class, and even to use new technologies to complete the task. One tool that is often used to support visual learning methods in the classroom is Inspiration Software (www.inspiration.com). Any learner may want to use this program to create professional-looking products, but Inspiration may be particularly useful for learners who have motor planning problems and require assistive technology to draw, design, or write.

Make A Mnemonic

If you took music lessons as a child, you likely still remember memorizing "Every Good Boy Does Fine" to remember the treble clef lines, EGBDF. If you think for a moment, you can probably remember other mnemonics that stuck with you during your school years and beyond. Your ability to recall this content is evidence that these tricks work, so hopefully you are already incorporating them into your lessons.

Mnemonics you can use to support all students include

> rhymes (e.g., "In 1492, Columbus sailed the ocean blue"),

> songs (e.g., "The 50 Nifty United States"),

> spellings (e.g., The principal is your pal),

> word associations (e.g., dessert has two esses because we always want more of it),

> acrostics (e.g., ROYGBIV = red, orange, yellow, green, blue, indigo, violet), and

> story chaining (creating a tale to link unrelated items).

Level It Out

To meet the needs of all students in your classroom, provide various ways to access the assigned text. Look for different versions of the book or chapter. *Romeo and Juliet*, for instance, is available in dozens of different formats. You can use the original play, annotated and modern-day language versions, graphic novels, and study guides. If you have students needing even more scaffolding, you can assign them to watch the play, a movie version of the play, or even a cartoon clip of the classic like this one created by the folks at SparkNotes: www.sparknotes.com/sparknotes/video/romeojuliet.

Another way to help all students access content at their own level is provide a range of texts focused on the same topic. If you are studying earthquakes, you might make available a picture book on the topic like *Earthquakes* by Seymour Simon, a leveled reader like *Earthquakes and Other Natural Disasters* by Harriet Griffey, a short newspaper clipping on a recent earthquake, or a compelling story about the potential impact of an earthquake, such as *Eight Days: A Story of Haiti* by Edwidge Danticat.

Hop, Skip, Or Roll Again

Make your classroom into a game board and let students play while they learn.

Tape off a tic-tac-toe board using duct tape. Have students play a game using their own bodies as pawns. Adapt it by having learners answer a question in order to move into a space.

Create a big trivia game using carpet squares as board spaces. Whenever students land on a certain color, they have to answer a question related to that color (e.g., red for math, green for science).

You might add unusual materials to make your games more interesting. Get large foam dice to move game pieces or people. Use pool noodles for a game of oversized pick up sticks. Draw on or otherwise decorate cork ceiling tiles to make a massive content-related memory game.

Give students different roles to play in both the creation and playing of the games. Some may want to develop the rules and others may want to lead the group in designing the board and related materials.

Cloud Their Learning

Word clouds are a visual representation of word frequency in a segment of text. The words that appear most often in the text show up in larger sizes than those appearing less frequently, so learners can easily see which words and themes are most relevant, or at least most repeated in a particular passage, section, chapter, speech, or book.

There are many ways to use word clouds in the classroom, so even if you have already been using them, consider trying a new application. If you typically use word clouds as a getting-to-know-you tool, feature them as a lead-in to a unit. If you have used them as a writing prompt, try introducing them to make predictions. Review this list of ideas for further inspiration:

> Create a word cloud of a document you will be examining and ask students to discuss themes they notice.

> Have students study a word cloud created from a chapter of fiction. Have them make predictions about the story.

> Invite students to make word cloud autobiographies. Then, have the class members guess which clouds belong to which students.

> Use clouds as a unique test review strategy. Give students clouds filled with words and terms they need to study.

> Ask students to make word cloud poetry.

> Have students share the themes of a speech they have just read. Then, put the text into a word cloud and have them compare the ideas they shared with the words that show up in the visual.

There are many websites that can be used to make your clouds; here are a few of the most popular:

> www.wordclouds.com

> www.wordle.net

> www.tagxedo.com

Notate & Collaborate

Consider offering a class wiki for the optional sharing of lecture notes. This type of support can be helpful in a variety of ways. First of all, many students find summarizing is useful in both organizing material and learning it. When students have an opportunity to take this a step further and share their work with others, it can be an incentive to not only complete summaries, but to complete them with care. Secondly, a shared notes page helps students understand the material from more than one perspective. Different students may highlight different examples and share different interpretations of the material. Finally, this tool will undoubtedly help students who need support not only with the content, but also with the task of note taking itself. A shared wiki can help struggling students learn what to highlight, how to organize material, and which strategies to use for outlining.

Take Note

Honor student differences by introducing a variety of note-taking methods into the classroom.

One of the most popular formats is the Cornell Notes system. This method involves dividing the notes page into three sections; students use most of the page to create two columns and draw a box or section at the bottom of the page. The right column is the space for general note taking. This is where the most important ideas should be recorded. The left area serves to complement the general area. This space is saved for annotation; students "comment on" their notes in this area. They add key words and clarify the concepts recorded in the right-hand column. This section may develop during the class itself or at the end of it. The section at the bottom of the page should be labeled "summary"; it is used to record the main ideas on that page.

The split-page method is very similar to the Cornell system. To create this type of system, students divide the page vertically into two sections—one for the main ideas and one for secondary ideas. This allows students to take notes while they organize concepts.

Mind mapping is a third option and is a technique that might appeal to visual learners. It requires students to arrange topics and ideas into circles, bubbles, and lines that connect to one another. This method invites students to make sense of the information as they are learning it.

In addition to these three, you can also offer students some informal note-taking options. You might allow them to take notes in pairs (one student writes down a comment and passes it to a partner, that student jots down a note and passes the paper back), let them take picture notes, or give them ideas for coding their written notes (e.g., put a ? beside their questions; put a ! beside ideas they deem most important).

See The Words

Visuwords (www.visuwords.com) is an "online graphical dictionary" where users can look up words to find their relationships to other words and phrases. The site produces diagrams in a mind-map format that show associations between words using color, shading, and symbols.

So, if a student types in the word, *monarchy*, he or she will see that it is a noun, that it is related to words like *kingdom* and *empire*, and that it is similar to *undemocratic*. The user can also hover over any of these words to get their definitions and click on any term to learn more about it. So, more clicks lead to a bigger word map, more information, and even more connections.

There are many uses for Visuwords in the classroom. You can use it to teach new words, explore word derivation, or learn about connections between words.

A lot of the information on this site would be found in a typical reference book or dictionary app, but the dynamic and playful nature of Visuwords makes it far more appealing to students than other dictionaries.

Make It Multi-Sensory

Do you work as part of a co-teaching team? If so, changing up your co-teaching structures is a must when it comes to UDL. One teach–one make multi-sensory is one of the most powerful co-teaching structures because it prompts educators to be creative.

In this structure, educators think beyond how to work together. One teach–one make multi-sensory might involve any number of experiences including demonstrations, presentations or creation of visuals, the addition of supportive audio cues or music, dramatic performances, and use of technology-related supports. Here are just a few specific ideas to help two educators meet the needs of learners using this model:

> One reads a passage from a book; one dramatically acts out the scene.

> One conducts a mini-lecture; one illustrates how to take notes on the interactive whiteboard.

> One conducts a mini-lecture; one holds up pictures/props to make concepts memorable.

> One conducts a mini-lecture; one leads a chant to emphasize targeted words/concepts.

> One teaches a lesson; one adds audio cues to make important points memorable.

> One teaches a lesson; one demonstrates a piece of assistive technology (e.g., a new app on a tablet).

Day 193

Read To Them

Teachers at every grade level should read to their students frequently, if not daily. Reading aloud fosters a sense of community in the classroom, provides common ground for discussion, entertains, requires little formal student response (giving all learners a time to feel confident and competent), and connects the group to reading as a way to learn.

Teachers of very young students will likely read many different selections each week. Teachers in middle school and high school, however, may not have the time to do a lot of reading aloud, but every educator should look for opportunities to share articles, blog posts, passages, newspaper excerpts, and short stories. A high school English teacher might read short passages from Natalie Goldberg's *Writing Down the Bones* before students begin a creative writing assignment. A social studies teacher might read an article from *The New York Times* (learning.blogs.nytimes.com/great-read-alouds-from-the-new-york-times) to teach current events.

To make the read aloud work well in a diverse classroom, be sure to read widely, feature selections across genres, and allow students to make suggestions.

Section III

Using UDL & Beyond

Ideology & Beliefs

Focus On Fair

In a UDL classroom, some learners may get materials or experiences that others do not. Some students will point out these perceived inequities and declare them unfair. For this reason, it is important to start the year by emphasizing that equal does not mean fair, and that no learner in the classroom will get the same things as his or her classmates. Some students, for instance, will get preferred seating, some will take tests in other environments, some will use e-readers, some will work with partners more often than others, some will use headphones to block out background noises during certain lessons, and some will need support from an ELL teacher. Use these examples as a starting point for communicating that you will always try to give students what they need, but that you will never treat them all the same.

 **Day 195**

Look For Competence

Teachers can look for competence and complexity in many ways—by helping an individual shine during a lesson, studying a student's learning style and teaching to it, or exploring how a learner expresses himself or herself and carving out a place in the classroom for that form of expression. Teachers looking for competence and complexity in learners should constantly consider the following questions:

› Who is this student?

› Under what circumstances does this student thrive?

› What gifts/skills/abilities does this student have?

› What is this student's awareness of himself or herself as a learner?

› What prevents me from seeing/helps me see this student's potential?

› How does this student learn?

› What does this student value?

› How and what can I learn from this student?

Day
196

Teach Up

UDL does not mean that you expect less from some students and more from others. It is true that you may need to adjust objectives for some, but this does not mean that you cannot appropriately challenge every learner in the classroom. It is a delicate balance, for sure, but all teachers must provide multiple means of representation, multiple means of engagement, and multiple means of action and expression without lowering expectations. A student who needs to use an audio book to finish a novel might still be able to handle very complex comprehension questions, and a learner who needs special seating, testing accommodations, clear examples, more personal support, and extra visuals may be the most talented mathematician in the class.

No matter how much support a student needs, it's imperative that expectations remain high. In the words of educator Douglas Biklen this means educators must "presume competence and go about the business of finding it".

Let Go

Give the students a little ownership of their learning. Demonstrate to students that you—as the teacher—are a part of the community of learners in the classroom and that they—as the students—are part of the teaching corps. There are several ways to "let go" in your UDL classroom including

> asking students to take on classroom responsibilities,

> offering choices,

> solving classroom problems collaboratively,

> teaming up with students on classroom management issues (e.g., seating chart, materials distribution), and

> surveying the class about learning preferences.

Day **198**

Mind Your Mindset

Children who adopt what psychologist Carol Dweck (2006) calls a growth mindset understand that intelligence isn't fixed but can be developed through effort. In her award-winning book on the topic, *Mindset*, Dweck explains that students who have a growth mindset are more willing to tackle challenges, learn from failure, and see criticism as useful feedback rather than a reason to give up.

Every classroom needs to encourage the growth mindset. UDL isn't just about meeting the needs of students; it is about challenging them to see and achieve their potential. Therefore, students in the UDL classroom regularly need to hear positive messages such as

> ˃ believe in yourself,
>
> ˃ embrace challenges,
>
> ˃ you can always improve,
>
> ˃ never stop trying, and
>
> ˃ use failure as a tool.

Ideology & Beliefs

Reject Average

If there is one word that prevents us from bringing our most creative work to the table in a UDL classroom, it is "average." No student in the classroom is truly typical. Every single learner brings a very unique collection of needs and abilities to their daily work, and we should always strive to uncover those needs and abilities. Further, we should explore ways to exploit each learner's gifts and challenge him or her to push a little more.

Reject "average". Prepare to be surprised, dazzled, and impressed by every student every day.

Invite Individuality

Recognize the uniqueness of your students. Get to know them. Find out their interests, goals, and values. Make notes on what is important to them. This type of knowledge is invaluable in the UDL classroom. It will help you choose instructional techniques, design curriculum, and provide individual feedback.

Day
201

See Parents As Partners

Build collaborative relationships with parents. Ask for input and suggestions. Invite them to share their expertise formally and informally. Bring them in to facilitate activities. Design volunteer opportunities beyond room parents and guest readers. Create a Twitter account to encourage communication and connection. Start a class blog to show off classroom events; invite parents as guest bloggers and encourage them to add comments. Call home regularly to share breakthroughs, achievements, and other good news.

Collaboration

Scout For Talent

Students bring many different talents and interests into our learning spaces every day. Study every learner in the classroom to identify these gifts, and try to capitalize on them daily in lessons. If you regularly scout for talent in your classroom, you will find many UDL partners who can make your lessons richer and more interesting.

You may want to identify one or more

> poets,

> classroom organizers/designers/decorators,

> illustrators/graphic notetakers,

> scribes,

> photographers,

> mobile app reviewers,

> historians,

> classroom exhibit curators,

> motivational quote finders/sharers,

> librarians, and

> mathematicians/statisticians.

Students in these roles can participate in lessons in any number of ways. They can lead learning stations, co-teach lessons with one or more teachers, or tutor or mentor other students.

Versions of these roles can be used at any grade level, and can be adopted for a few lessons, or for an entire quarter, semester, or year.

Customize Conferences

In a universally-designed school or classroom, every norm and practice should be evaluated to ensure that students can succeed across activities and learning experiences. Family-teacher conferences are no exception and should be designed for maximum participation.

Ideas for customizing conferences include

> giving families a choice of where to meet (e.g., at the school or at a community center);

> making the seating, lighting, and environment as welcoming as possible;

> offering coffee and snacks;

> extending conference times for some or all families;

> having students make videos to greet their families and to share their own evaluation of their learning to date;

> giving families written material to review in advance so the session can focus on discussing the student's progress; and

> asking families to submit one or two questions prior to the conference so these can be given priority.

Another way to create a more dynamic and effective conference experience is to involve your students. During such meetings, teachers present their own comments, but they also listen, encourage, and informally teach students how to conduct a conference, and how to talk about their abilities and their needs. This practice builds self-advocacy skills and helps learners and their families get on the same page about learning goals, progress, and challenges.

Help Them Help You

Help families to help your work in the classroom.

Share your goals with parents. Be explicit about what students should know and be able to do at the end of each quarter, semester, and year. Explain the standards. Post vocabulary lists for the year on your class blog. Show them work samples.

Provide tips about materials and activities that they can access to bolster in-class learning. Encourage them to build their home libraries. Show them free apps that can be used to support homework. Recommend board and card games that help students build skills.

Post short videos on YouTube to teach parents specific ways to support their children. Do you want kindergarteners to practice social skills like sharing and working collaboratively? Give a few tips about teaching those competencies. Do you need your middle school families to support organization skills and independence? Provide guidance on how to do just that.

Day 205

Volunteer For Volunteers

It is a wonder how underutilized classroom volunteers are in schools that seem to need them most. No resource will help you in your UDL quest more than people, so all schools committed to meeting the needs of all learners should seriously consider the benefits of building a solid volunteer corps. Use it to create materials (e.g., visual supports), work with students directly, or even to provide seminars or mini-lectures a few times a year.

Invite Them To The Teacher's Table

Do your students know what UDL is? They should. Students can be allies for you in meeting learning needs but it will be hard for them to do so if they do not have the necessary language and knowledge. Teach students the language of Universal Design for Learning, multiple intelligences, growth mindset, and so on. Talk to them throughout the year about how you reach and teach all students. In some instances, it may even be appropriate to let older students read professional literature on UDL.

Invite Observation

Ask a trusted colleague to observe a lesson and provide feedback on your teaching. Have them focus specifically on one aspect of your instruction, such as an element of UDL. Possible observation targets include

> emphasizing/reinforcing lesson objectives,

> pacing a lesson appropriately,

> integrating assistive technology into a lesson,

> using total physical response (TPR) strategies,

> providing multiple means of expression,

> encouraging student exploration/questioning,

> creating opportunities for students with disabilities to participate in a classroom discussion,

> using specific feedback, and

> encouraging peer interaction/support.

Role Share

Assess what the different adults in your building do and do not do on an average day. Ask the following questions:

> Do all adults take responsibility for all students?

> Do all adults feel comfortable providing support to all students?

> Are teachers working together to meet the needs of students?

> Are any of the talents of the adults in this building being wasted?

> Are we duplicating roles and responsibilities where we should be delegating and distributing roles and responsibilities?

Discuss responses with staff members and facilitate a conversation about how adults can work together to teach all learners more effectively.

Co-Teach With Students

Appoint a student to be the co-teacher of the day. This student can take notes as you lecture, read aloud to the group, and help with paperwork and other classroom tasks. Some students can even be assigned more challenging tasks, such as developing mini-lessons or creating models, metaphors, or complex examples to teach a concept.

Have A Board Meeting

The next time you are at the helm of the classroom, taking notes on the board, try flipping this process and bringing your students up to do the work.

First, determine what you want students to do. They might be asked to solve a problem, create a diagram, list ideas, or brainstorm via a mind map. Then, have the class come to the front of the room, give each student a small section of the board and direct them to work on the same task simultaneously. If your dry erase board is not very big, post chart paper around the room to create additional work areas, or have students work with partners and share the board space.

Use this technique as a way to quickly assess student learning and to encourage students to teach and learn from one another.

Delegate

We often underestimate the capacity of our students to be self-sufficient and to support one another. Create a robust and responsive learning environment in your classroom by turning management over to your students. This practice fosters responsibility, makes the day run more smoothly, and helps learners become independent—an important goal on its own. Students can pass out folders and other materials, critique one another's work, move furniture for different activities and groupings, keep records of their own work, chart their progress by using established goals, help design some of their own tasks, and make suggestions for smoother classroom operation.

Go Home

If you have a student with unique challenges on your class list, consider making a home visit to observe him or her in a familiar place and to learn from family members. A home visit will help you learn more about the student's support system, her hobbies and interests, and even some of her daily challenges. You may find that one student has many brothers and sisters who may serve as reading partners or homework helpers. You may learn that another can play the piano, loves to make card houses, or goes to Renaissance fairs. Any of these pieces of information could be helpful in supporting students and designing appropriate learning experiences for them.

Home visits may be used for any student, but they may be especially helpful for those learners who have communication challenges and cannot easily relay information about home and family, including those who are learning English, those with disabilities, and those who are very anxious or shy.

Switch It Up

Are you a general educator who has never created sensory supports for students with disabilities? Are you a special educator who has never designed enrichment activities for all learners? Are you an occupational therapist who has never taught a small-group lesson in a general education classroom? Are you an administrator who has never directly supported a student with multiple disabilities? If you can answer "yes" to one of these questions, you may want to explore a new role in your classroom or school.

In a school dedicated to UDL, teachers look for ways to learn from colleagues. One way to do that is to occasionally swap responsibilities with others on your team. Even if you only do this a few times a year, it will help you build skills and communicate to all learners that every staff member in their school is there to support every student in their school.

Expand The Staff

Help students build their own personal learning networks. Talk to them about what it means to have a network, what they want to learn, and how to cultivate and build a community that will support and inspire them and their work. Students can learn from their peers, older or younger students, other teachers, school therapists, administrators, parents and other family members, and even from those they interact with online like virtual pen pals and long-distance mentors.

Just Ask

Don't be afraid to ask students for help as you work to provide each of them with the most customized educational experience possible. If you are stuck on how to appropriately assess a particular learner, consider asking him or her for ideas. If you can't seem to find a way to motivate students during the last period of the day, survey them to learn about their favorite and least favorite lessons so far, along with their ideas for keeping daily work interesting.

Collaboration

Solicit Stories

It is important to allow students to share their interests, likes and dislikes, needs and struggles as much as possible.

One way to do this is to invite learners to craft and share their stories. Learning students' stories can help you personalize instruction and create a closer-knit classroom community. You can set up a story slam in your classroom, invite students to write short autobiographies, or even ask them to create mini-documentaries of their lives.

Open Your Door

Invite families into the classroom whenever possible. Use their expertise in your units. Have them facilitate small groups. Feature them as guest readers. Put them on panels. Ask them to talk about their hobbies, their work, and their interests. Bring them in to help supervise art, design, and project-based lessons.

Families can help us meet learner needs in three important ways. For starters, as they work in our schools and classrooms, they get to know more about curriculum, instruction, and assessment. In so doing, they can give us helpful and informed feedback about how their children can learn best. For instance, they may see their child struggling in a cooperative group and suggest peers who may work with their son or daughter more effectively. Secondly, family members who work in classrooms may gain a richer understanding of what they can do at home to help their child succeed in school. Parents who visit and volunteer during reading lessons, for instance, will likely learn new strategies for addressing comprehension and fluency goals. Finally, families can help you meet diverse student needs by providing different perspectives and another set of hands in your classroom. Family members free educators to work with small groups, give individual help to students, and offer observations that may lead to new insights, ideas, or supports.

There are so many benefits to opening your classroom door to families. So, don't just invite them. Advertise. Remind them. Encourage them. Assure them they are welcome.

Split The Class

Co-teach during all or part of the day? Instead of co-teaching in a tag team formation, try splitting the class in two, with each of you delivering a lesson to half the group. This parallel teaching format gives all students more teacher attention, and provides educators with opportunities to question, observe, and offer feedback to a smaller group of learners.

There are many ways to split the class and meet learner needs using this model:

› Two teachers can teach the same content at the same time.

› Two teachers can assess students using two different tools or instruments at the same time.

› Two teachers can teach different but related content at the same time (e.g., Axis Powers/Allied Forces); groups then switch, and the teachers can teach the lessons again to the new groups.

› Two teachers can lead a discussion on the same topic with different groups.

› One teacher can teach a lesson while the other conducts a review session; groups can then switch, so the teachers can repeat their lessons with the new groups.

› Two teachers can conduct the same experiment, demonstration, or skit.

Cross Over

Look into bringing cross-age tutors into your classroom. Older students can offer a number of supports for younger students and often benefit from doing so. Cross-age tutors might be charged with supporting the classroom in any number of ways including

> listening to readers share favorite books;

> reading to students;

> having conversations in a target language;

> helping with homework;

> leading a musical instrument practice session;

> reviewing with flashcards, partner games, or Q & A;

> mentoring in a specific skill (e.g., organization, studying);

> writing collaboratively; and

> teaching students to use new apps, computer games, or technology tools.

Get Mentors

A powerful way to provide enrichment while connecting students to the community is to provide mentors. Mentors might work with some or all learners to help them understand real-world applications of their studies and, in many cases, to introduce work that provides another level of challenge.

Mentors are different from tutors in that they may not teach anything directly. Instead, they serve as coaches or advocates for those needing direction, inspiration, or advice.

Mentors can be adults that work inside (e.g., a psychologist mentoring a student interested in brain research), or outside (e.g., a local artist mentoring a student interested in photography) the building. A mentor can also be an older student. An older child with ADHD might serve as a mentor for a younger child with the same diagnosis, for example.

Assign A Scribe

Permit a partner to scribe or write for a learner who cannot write or express himself or herself easily on paper. Scribes can be used for any writing assignment, including journaling and writer's workshop activities. In some cases, a scribe will merely record everything his or her partner says. In other situations, however, the scribe may be asked to contribute a bit more. He or she may even engage in a little collaborative writing.

Scribes can also be used to take a set of model notes for some or all peers. While all the students may be responsible for taking their own notes, a scribe can occasionally be assigned to create a detailed outline to be used as a supplement for those who may struggle to write quickly or to organize their thoughts in writing.

You can assign a scribe based on fastidiousness or on ability to take the most complete set of notes. You can also assign someone who might create a study tool that is useful in its uniqueness. A scribe who likes to take visual notes, diagram ideas, and map concepts with color and images might be as smart a choice as the one who covers pages with observations, facts, and lists and never misses a detail. Or you can assign them both the job and feature two sets of notes on your classroom blog or wiki.

Team With The Therapist

Related service providers can do more than support students with physical, sensory, and communication needs. They can design instruction and provide ideas that will help both students with identified needs and those without. Therefore, it is imperative that educators collaborate with these professionals for the purpose of UDL. Teachers should, for instance, offer vocabulary lists from upcoming units to speech and language pathologists, or talk to occupational therapists about ways they may support all students in reaching new writing standards.

Share The Spotlight

There are so many benefits to co-teaching. Students typically experience a wider range of lesson formats in the co-taught classroom, and they get to learn from two different perspectives. In addition, teachers gain on-the-spot professional development as they observe their colleague's techniques and work with them.

Many teachers would like to reap the benefits of co-teaching, but they simply do not have the time or resources to do so. This does not mean, however, that teaming up with another teacher is out of the question; it simply indicates that a little creativity is needed.

One of the best ways to team when a full co-teaching model is out of reach is to use what I call "spotlight" co-teaching. In this model, two teachers choose one part of the day or week as a focus, and together they co-plan and co-teach during that segment for one day, a few weeks, or an entire year. I call it spotlight co-teaching because it allows teams to work together to "shine a light" on and problem solve around a single activity, routine, or task (e.g., the administration of spelling tests, morning meetings, math review time). The co-teaching is not intended to serve as an ongoing support (although it might), but as an opportunity to generate new ideas, materials, and strategies that can be implemented by just one teacher once the segment is no longer collaboratively taught.

Spotlight co-teaching can be undertaken by any number of professionals on your team. Therapists, social workers, school psychologists, administrators, and coaches can all be invited to co-teach and engage in follow-up brainstorming.

Think Beyond 1:1

If you have paraprofessionals assigned to one or two students in your classroom, talk to your building administrators about how to make the most out of this support. Paraprofessionals are typically hired to provide assistance, and make curriculum and instruction more accessible for one or more targeted students. Too often, this focus on a few causes learned helplessness and can result in some students getting more cues, guidance, and direct support than they need.

So, what is a better use of paraprofessional support? Use these valuable educators to help in creating more accessible and welcoming classrooms. Yes, most paraprofessionals will need to provide direct supports to individual students at certain times, but when that is not necessary or appropriate, look for ways that his or her talents can create support for all. Can this educator take visual notes during a lecture; help all students with individual projects; facilitate small group instruction; provide check-in supports for students needing extra help; or collect data on a few, some, or all students? These ideas not only make the most of a valuable resource, but they can provide indirect support to students with disabilities and unique learning profiles.

Buddy Up

In her groundbreaking book *The Dreamkeepers* (1994), Gloria Ladson-Billings highlights the work of a teacher who insists on collaboration and asks students to buddy up and support one another from the first day of school. She shares that she commonly talks to student partners when learners are struggling. She reminds them that they are part of a community and need to help one another. According to the teacher, it works: "Within a couple of months I begin to see them looking out for one another. One student will hesitate before he turns in his paper and will go check to make sure the buddy is doing okay" (p. 72). This type of reciprocal support can teach responsibility and create a sense of cooperation in the classroom.

If you think this idea can work in your classroom, you might assign long-term learning partners who work together to review, study, teach, and support one another, or you can switch your partners regularly and strategically based on the difficulty, content, and demands of lessons.

Let Them Plan

Let students be in charge by providing them with personalized learning agendas for a segment of the day or for a particular lesson (Kluth & Danaher, 2013). Agendas allow students to set their own goals and choose their own activities.

Resembling pages of a daily planner or calendar, personalized learning agendas are essentially blank schedules broken into small chunks of time (10- or 15-minute blocks). This tool allows the student to plan activities for each segment. In other words, an agenda allows a student to write his or her own lesson plan.

As you begin to use agendas, be sure that students have clear lists of activities to choose from (e.g., engage in research, work on a lab with a partner, finish notes) as well as guidance on how to best use their time. In addition, you will want to sign off on their plans before they begin working.

Technology

Day 227

Snap To It

Every day there seems to be a new app that educators are raving about, but few are as versatile as the camera. The camera app is easy for any learner to use, and has the potential to "shake up" classroom instruction in a variety of ways. You can have students snap photos to

> create visual essays,

> add to their blog posts,

> create graphics for presentations,

> respond to questions,

> prompt writing,

> capture observations,

> collect evidence of a problem/phenomenon,

> illustrate cause and effect,

> assemble story boards,

> "gather" items during a scavenger hunt,

> supplement descriptions in a lab notebook, and

> create products for the class or community (e.g., tourism guides, yearbook, greeting cards).

Day 228

Integrate AAC

Students who cannot speak or who do not have reliable ways to express themselves may use augmentative and alternative communication (AAC) to replace or supplement their speech. If you have students with this need in your classroom, you will want to make sure that you gain proficiency with their communication systems and carve out space for them to be heard.

Look for opportunities for these students to comment, question, and offer ideas. They will use their communication systems to complete work and connect with peers and staff, of course, but you will also want to provide them with time to practice skills during whole-class and small-group lessons. Encourage these students to use their communication systems to

> share the date, weather, or schedule changes;

> offer a fact, joke, or reminder of the day;

> ask or answer discussion questions;

> ask a "planted question" (a question that has been programmed into the system by the teacher);

> define vocabulary words;

> choose a book, activity, or game for the class;

> share a relevant quote or passage; or

> add sound effects to a story or skit.

Technology

Offer Handwriting Alternatives

Many students shut down when asked to put pencil to paper. Some learners with disabilities have motor planning problems and struggle mightily with handwriting. Their written work may take a long time to complete and may be illegible or hard to read at best. Others simply cannot produce much or any text via handwriting due to physical disabilities.

To support these students, offer tools that will help them complete written work without excessive challenges. Students might be offered tablets or computers so they can type their work. They can also be given speech-to-text apps or programs to use. Finally, you can let these learners provide verbal responses from time to time. They can either work with a teacher to provide those answers or submit an audio or video recording of their work.

Day 230

Form A Response

Looking for an alternative to exit slips and classroom clickers? You need Formative (goformative.com).

Instead of calling on individual learners to answer whole-class questions, have them all share at once using 1:1 devices. Formative allows you to quickly assess students' understanding of content, and provide feedback. You can do so using a points system or by providing written comments.

Day 231

Spark Their Interest

Many teachers know about Spark Notes (www.sparknotes.com) but may not have considered the many ways it can be a tool for UDL. The free notes on this site help struggling readers better understand assigned literature, and the related tools allow teachers to easily adapt text, assessments, and other materials. Parents can also can use the site to assist their kids with homework so be sure to let them know about this helpful tool.

Day 232

Tune In

You have probably already visited Teaching Channel (www.teachingchannel.com) and accessed their huge collection of lesson clips, but consider revisiting the site to view an old favorite or a new clip. Choose from dozens of topics, including how to use data walls, computer math games, learning menus, and questioning techniques in a UDL classroom.

I have viewed dozens of these (many more than once) and have shared several of them with audiences during staff development presentations. They are perfect for those times when you want a bit more information on a new technique but don't have a lot of time to spare. They are bite-sized (about 7-10 minutes each) and smartly edited to show both teacher perspectives and classroom illustrations.

Day 233

Get Glogging

The next time your students make posters, check out Glogster (edu.glogster.com) as an alternative to cutting, pasting, and stenciling. This site lets students create an interactive visual using text, images, music, and video.

Encourage students to work collaboratively to create their products. Some learners will love creating the visual itself, others will enjoy looking for relevant video clips, and still others will be interested in creating the text that ties it all together.

Glogs work well as formative assessments or as alternatives to traditional study-and-review tasks.

Put Up The Powerpoint

Many educators use PowerPoint or other presentation software for daily lectures and whole-class lessons. These programs are useful in a UDL classroom because they allow educators to create lecture materials once and refine them over time as audiences change and content needs to be revised. Additionally, creating note sets for students is a breeze with PowerPoint; it's as easy as hitting the print or send button.

Want other ideas for creating great visual presentations? Check out Haiku Deck (www.haikudeck.com), Prezi (www.prezi.com), Emaze (www.emaze.com), and Animoto (www.animoto.com) for appealing alternatives to PowerPoint.

Visit My Blog

To learn more about UDL, visit my professional blog: www.paulakluth.com. There you will find blog posts and articles about a range of topics related to Universal Design for Learning including inclusive education, differentiated instruction, responsive class-rooms, and co-teaching/collaboration. You will also find a "tip of the day" at the top of the page and several short articles to download and share.

Day 236

Phone It In

So many teachers are taking advantage of the fact that increasing numbers of students have access to iPads and cellphones in the classroom. These devices work well as tools for the UDL classroom, so embrace the fact that you may have to tolerate random ringtones and start dialing up a phone-based lesson or two.

For starters, you might have students use phones as

> augmentative communication supports,

> blogging tools,

> dictionaries and thesauruses,

> sources for gathering and editing photos for projects,

> data collection tools,

> calculators,

> organizers, and

> translation aids.

Day 237

Make Reading Work

ReadWorks (www.readworks.org) is a free website that every teacher should bookmark on the computer. It features hundreds of lesson plans and more than two thousand non-fiction and fiction passages aligned to Common Core standards. Use this site to find reading selections that are appropriately challenging for every student in your classroom.

Learn In A Flash

Have you visited Headmagnet (www.headmagnet.com)? You can use the site to post your own sets of flashcards or just to study the sets others have posted. This site is a great test prep tool and has a lot of homework-help potential. It tracks both study time and learning progress. It also allows educators to personalize review time. For instance, you can post different vocabulary lists or sets of facts for different learning levels, grade levels, or interest areas and allow students to sample from any of the lists.

Day 239

Babble A Bit

Check out Fotobabble (www.fotobabble.com) and begin imagining the possibilities for your classroom. This simple tool lets you add your voice to any photograph. The uses for classrooms are endless. How about having learners create a poem to comment on a photo they have taken? Or letting them snap a picture that represents a time or place in history and narrate it as a notable figure from that era? Math teachers can also make use of this tool as students can photograph multi-step problems on paper or a dry erase board and engage in a voice-over explanation of the steps they took to solve it.

You can use Fotobabble to support several different skills and competencies. For example, students might use it to practice communication skills such as vocalizing or speaking confidently in a target language.

Day **240**

Take Off To NASA

Trying to build background knowledge in your classroom? Virtual field trips offered on the websites of NASA (virtualfieldtrip. jpl.nasa.gov), Discovery (www.discoveryeducation.com/Events/virtual-field-trips/explore), and even The White House (www.whitehouse.gov/about/inside-white-house/interactive-tour) can provide your students with a unique learning experience. The beauty of these virtual fieldtrips is that they can be watched several times by those who are really interested in the content or by those who need repetition in order to learn.

Want even more links to virtual learning? Check out a huge collection of video links on the fabulous resource-rich blog, Tech for Teachers (techforteachers.com/teachers/virtual-field-trips).

Day 241

Flip For Flip Books

Have a little fun in your classroom with student-created flip books. Flip books are interactive graphic organizers that help students write, organize, and retain information. They can be used in any subject and with just about any topic.

Students can use flip books to take notes, collect facts, or explore new content. They can write math stories, illustrate a scientific principle, or retell a historical event.

Once they have tried creating their own cut-and-paste flip books, you might want to show them how to create virtual versions. Check out PageFlip-Flap (www.pageflip-flap.com) and Flipsnak (www.flipsnack.com) for ideas.

Day 242

Listen Up

Today, there are so many ways for students to listen and learn. They can pop on headphones and tune into podcasts on topics ranging from oil spills to grammar rules to photography. If you like this idea but are not sure where to find appropriate material, check out Listenwise (www.listenwise.com). Listenwise helps teachers bring authentic voices and non-fiction stories to the classroom. They curate public radio to help teachers access high-quality content and to inspire students to learn from listening. The free subscription gets you the podcasts, but the paid subscription provides access to lesson plans, interactive transcripts, and even reduced audio speed for those needing it.

Do you have students who wouldn't be interested in listening to podcasts? Engage them in creating these tools instead of accessing them. Students can create podcasts to:

› teach a concept or skill to fellow students;

› present original opinion pieces, short stories, or one-act plays;

› broadcast a classroom discussion on a current event;

› showcase their developing skills in a target language; or

› interview one another on topics related to current or upcoming units.

Day 243

Read, Write & Think

ReadWriteThink (www.readwritethink.org) provides teachers with information on the highest quality practices in reading and language arts instruction. Partners with The International Reading Association, The National Council of Teachers of English, and The Verizon Foundation, the organization provides a range of free standards-based materials such as printable graphic organizers and writing checklists. They also have interactive tools, including fill-in-the-blank diamanté poem frames, KWL creators, and word family sorts.

Use this site to download teaching tools and lesson plans that encourage students to learn in a variety of ways.

Fold-A-Lesson

Excite your project-loving learners by letting them build, create, and craft today. Canon's Creative Park (cp.c-ij.com/en/) provides directions for creating stunning paper models of many science- and social studies-related items, including globes, sundials, and hydroelectric power plants.

Use these models to introduce a new topic, to bring an area of study to life, or to encourage collaboration or teamwork. You can also use them to provide all students with a visual support for a particular unit or lesson.

They are many ways to customize these materials and activities for the different types of learners in your classroom. There are so many models here that you could allow students to make choices based on their strengths and abilities. You can also offer support by completing parts of the model for or with students. Finally, you could respond to student differences by asking some learners to design a standards-based paper model of their own.

Read With The Stars

Storyline Online (www.storylineonline.net) is a unique website sponsored by the Entertainment Industry Foundation. The site is populated by videos of Screen Actors Guild members reading popular children's books. The videos include close-ups of the actors reading, soft music, images from the books themselves, and a little bit of discussion about the text. Each book comes with a resource guide that teachers can download to access discussion points and activities.

This site can be used to let students gain access to repeated readings of books, to become familiar with a text before reading it, and to hear models of fluent reading. It can also help learners access books they cannot easily access on their own, and teach them about the behaviors associated with fluent reading (e.g., reading with expression).

See The Signs

The American Sign Language Browser (commtechlab.msu.edu/sites/aslweb/browser.htm) provides videos of hundreds of words and phrases. Use this tool to teach students learning sign language, and to find visuals you can use in the classroom to quickly, quietly, and easily give directions, and communicate with individual learners.

You can also use sign to quietly communicate with the entire class. For instance, you may want to learn the signs for *yes, no, quiet please, find a partner, thank you, line up,* and *clean up.* Other words/phrases like *fantastic, interesting, wonderful, wow, keep it up,* and *let's go* can be used with all students and can be taught to learners to use with one another. Many students can "catch" visual commands more easily than they do verbal commands, so adding visual language often helps classroom management. Another benefit of using ASL in the classroom is that some students with and without disabilities may get hooked and decide they want to learn the language.

There are many other sites that can be used to learn and teach ASL. Take a look at one or more of them to get ideas for your classroom:

> www.aslpro.com

> www.lifeprint.com

> www.start-american-sign-language.com

Experiment With Experiments

Veritasium (veritasium.com) is a fantastic science video blog that features posts on a range of topics, including gravity, inertia, force, and atoms.

The goal of this blog is to make scientific ideas accessible and interesting. The site's short films can be used in the classroom and reviewed at home for extended study of certain concepts and ideas. Some students may be responsible for watching videos and answering questions about them, while others can be assigned to repeat the site's fun-filled experiments (e.g., Slinky Drop, Exploding Drum) or even to make their own related video clips.

Day 248

View The Elements

Periodic Visuals (www.periodicvideos.com) is a clever website featuring videos for each one of the 118 elements. So many students who struggle in science need this type of support. Some will react to the humor in the clips. Others will enjoy seeing the experiments that they might not experience in a classroom setting. And still others will benefit from the featured illustrations and explanations.

Day 249

Caption It

Most DVDs and many video clips available on educational websites allow users to add captions. Teachers should always choose this option even if students in the classroom do not have an obvious need for it, as some learners may profit from the captions even when they are not aware that they do. Captions are beneficial for students who are Deaf or hard of hearing, those with reading disabilities, those with attention challenges, and those who have difficulty filtering out background noise.

Day 250

Face It

You probably use Facebook (www.facebook.com) in your personal life, but have you tried it in the classroom? There are hundreds of ways to creatively use this social media platform, or others like it.

You can

- facilitate a classroom book club;

- create and support study groups;

- assess students' social media etiquette skills;

- celebrate student work;

- offer homework help and reminders;

- engage in collaborative brainstorming sessions; or

- dialogue with a content-related guest speaker such as a young adult (YA) author, a favorite cartoonist, or a local scientist.

Day 251

Flip Out

Flipping the classroom means switching the typical equation of listening to a lecture or presentation at school and completing individual work at home. Teachers in flipped classrooms provide lecture content online and then allow students to engage with that material in some way during class time. In this model, the teacher does not need to be at the helm of the classroom for long periods of time and is, therefore, free to work with individual students, support small groups, and assess work for most or all of a class period.

There are many reasons to use flipped lessons in mixed-ability classrooms. They allow presentations of content to be viewed repeatedly, let teachers spend class time coaching and supporting instead of delivering material, and—when students are invited to help in the creation of the videos—provide them with opportunities to both teach and learn.

If you feel overwhelmed by the idea of flipping, start by using it for just a lesson or two. In addition, experiment with using it in different ways and to teach different types of material. You may not view it as a great match for review sessions, but end up seeing benefits for some of your daily lessons.

Day 252

Keep Up On Tech

Don't be afraid of the newest gadgets on the scene. You may not jump in and use everything that becomes available, but try to make a habit of trying a new tool each month, either in your planning and teaching, or in the classroom for student use. For instance, you might have students make digital shorts with iPads, try their hands at creating timelines using Popplet (www.popplet.com), or use Google Earth (www.google.com/earth) to explore the planet. Try an Instagram-inspired lesson (www.instagram.com), use Go-Animate (www.goanimate.com) to add humor to a lecture, and explore a variety of lesson planning apps with your fellow teachers.

Need help in this area? Ask your students for recommendations on tech tools that they would like to use in the classroom.

Day 253

Offer Annotation Options

Students need strategies for note taking that do not add exponentially to their workload. Providing them with tips on how to highlight and annotate can make a big impact on their success. Students may need to know what to highlight (e.g., important passages, unfamiliar vocabulary words, key quotes, relevant themes/ideas) or how to highlight (e.g., ? = question or unsure of meaning; * = important; [ ] = quotable; ___ = new vocabulary). They may also need to know how to make use of the margins. Many learners don't know they can use this space to add definitions, note questions, summarize, or add predictions.

As more teachers begin to supplement and replace traditional texts with digital texts, it is important that students learn how to organize, process, and share online resources as well. One tool that can be used for this purpose is Diigo (www.diigo.com). It's easy to learn and can be used for highlighting, annotating, bookmarking, and sharing digital texts.

Spell Their Way

Do you have students who love games? Some who need to hear cues as opposed to see them? Others who like repetition? Have them all practice at VocabularySpellingCity (www.spellingcity.com).

The site is user-friendly for all learning levels and ages. To use it, students enter spelling words and then choose from a variety of activities to learn them such as finding the missing letter in a word, alphabetizing lists, or writing sentences. Learners can even give themselves a practice test.

This site can provide a variety of supplements to paper-and-pencil homework assignments. It is also a great choice for motivating spellers who are preparing for a competition.

Power Up

Looking for fresh ideas for early finishers or for those who need an on-the-spot UDL solution? Have students

› use Quia (www.quia.com) to compose a puzzle on the current topic of study;

› work on the class website;

› search for wallpaper or a screen saver related to the content;

› create a PowToon (www.powtoon.com) product related to the topic of study;

› take a virtual field trip related to the subject matter;

› create a digital scrapbook about the lesson;

› assemble a hot list based on common unit-related questions;

› have a dialogue about the material with a peer via texting or Twitter; or

› make a short presentation using Blabberize (www.blabberize.com), VoiceThread (www.voicethread.com), ShowMe (www.showme.com), or another similar tool.

Day 256

Go On A Quest

If you are looking for more options for student-directed learning, look no further than the WebQuest. A WebQuest (Dodge, 1995) is a collaborative, inquiry-oriented lesson format in which most or all the information that students access comes from the internet.

This lesson format is designed to make web learning efficient. A typical web search involves as many misses as hits. That is, some sites that students find may be reputable and have the information they need, and others may not. In a WebQuest, surfing is not necessary; students skip the browsing process and spend their time on the web reading, learning, and creating.

To set up a WebQuest, simply pose problems for teams of students to solve and then direct them to research solutions online. The process is intended to encourage students to explore a wide range of perspectives, materials, and resources, and to inspire them to think differently, learn more authentically, and potentially even create products that spark new questions. For example, Cynthia Matzat's Radio Days (www.thematzats.com/radio) takes students back in time to the 1930s and '40s by having them create a radio play. By connecting directly to sound clips, broadcast, and radio scripts, students have enough structure to be successful in the task, but plenty of freedom to create a unique product.

Visit www.webquest.org for lesson ideas, resources, and more information on this method.

Release The Dragon

Speech recognition software like Dragon Naturally Speaking is an assistive technology tool that many students find motivating. Speech recognition tools can generate excitement for writing, especially for students who struggle with assignments due to learning disabilities, physical disabilities, or other challenges. Students without disabilities may also be interested in trying Dragon Naturally Speaking or other tools simply because they are new and different.

Let all students try speech recognition software to

> create on-the-spot dialogue;

> write music lyrics;

> brainstorm/create a short list of ideas;

> dictate observations during an experiment, project, or performance; or

> write a letter.

Day 258

Be Manipulative

The National Library of Virtual Manipulatives (nlvm.usu.edu/en/nav/vlibrary.html) is a National Science Foundation–supported project that began nearly two decades ago. The goal was to develop a library of interactive, web-based virtual manipulatives for teaching and learning mathematics. Students can work with spinners, create bar graphs, build patterns with virtual blocks, and more.

The tools featured are great for visual learners; the site offers a novel way for students to check their work and create concrete models of abstract concepts.

Day 259

Let Them Blog

Blogs are not only a great way for teachers to share information and learn from one another, they are also a unique tool for encouraging communication, writing, and reading. Students who are less than motivated about writing often show interest in generating content for an authentic audience and receiving feedback from those far and away.

Even young students and those with very little writing ability can blog. Students with significant disabilities might create wordless posts by selecting or taking appropriate photos for the blog. Students who are very tech-savvy may want to write posts as well as work on promoting the blog or designing it.

A classroom blog may exist for many reasons. It might be used to share information, connect students to the world beyond the classroom, or promote learning about digital citizenship.

Student blogs can also be used in the classroom. Individuals might create blogs to explore and share a fascination or interest (e.g., American politics, cosplay, basketball), engage in a long-term project (e.g., watching 20 books based on novels) , or get feedback on work.

To use blogging in the classroom, start by choosing an appropriate blogging platform. Talk to the technology support teachers in your district about which one is the best for your students, their ages, and your purposes. Then, let your administrators and families know what you are doing. Share your objectives and your plans for use with them. After you are ready to begin, set rules with your students. They will need to be aware of issues such as cyber-bullying and copyright infringement. Finally, choose when and how your learners will blog. Will it be a center or station that all students in the classroom access at some point? Will it always occur during your language arts block or will students be allowed to blog across the school day?

Day
260

Go Antique Shopping

When most of us think of technology, the slickest new tools come to mind. While it is important to explore the newest apps, software, and hardware, consider that old-school gadgets and gizmos may be very appealing to some of your students. Have a student who is not particularly excited about math apps? Introduce an adding machine. Supporting a reluctant writer? Try a typewriter or desktop word processor.

A middle school teacher I observed hooked her students on writing dialogue by distributing old tape recorders and microphones and allowing them time to converse, record their chatter, and develop scripts based on their recordings. And a fifth-grade teacher I met used a Rolodex to display vocabulary words for a student who loved the idea of using "real" office supplies to study.

Day 261

Skype

While Skype was not designed as an educational tool, it's quickly becoming one as teachers discover how it can enrich their lessons. Even something as simple as chatting with a mentor through a video call can add excitement to a lesson.

Use Skype to make learning more interesting, visit new places, and connect with people related to classroom content. You can integrate it into lessons in the following ways:

> Invite guest speakers (e.g., authors, experts, grandparents/seniors who have lived through historical moments).

> Invite guest readers (e.g., family members).

> Talk to a native speaker of a language that students are studying.

> Take a virtual field trip (e.g., park, museum).

> Visit pen pals.

> Visit parents in the workplace to explore careers and the community.

> Play mystery Skype with your learners by calling other classrooms and having the class guess what city, state, or country they are calling.

All of these ideas can be used for one or two students, several learners, or the entire classroom.

#Hash It Out

Use hashtags in the classroom to support your tech-savvy students and to expand learning beyond classroom walls. You could create a hashtag for a class (e.g., #OakParkBio9; #MsParkersReaders) or a topic (e.g., #Jupiterquestions; #filmmaking101; #1900sWisconsin; #mathintherealworld).

Hashtags can create a sense of community with your group or groups as learners can connect around the clock and efficiently share their thoughts, notes, and observations with classmates. Hashtags can also give students access to more resources. Teachers can respond to student questions and posts, but so can educators, family members, topic experts, authors, and other students. Finally, hashtags can serve as a way to introduce students to learning via social media. Many students use hashtags to learn about their favorite singers/bands, television shows, and sports teams, but not all Twitter enthusiasts know how to use it to learn a new skill, get information, or dialogue with others to gain knowledge and competencies.

Plan To Build

Build great lessons in a snap by visiting the plan exchange on the CAST website (udlexchange.cast.org/home). This dynamic planning tool prompts users to create lessons appropriate for students with diverse learning profiles. There are spaces for lesson openings, closings, assessments, objectives, and more. Further, there are reminders to consider the needs of all. The materials section, for instance, features this question: "What options have you included in lesson materials and supplies that address the variability of learners?"

And that's not all! You can use this tool to browse lesson plans created by other users. You can adopt the plans you find or simply get ideas for tweaking the ones you are creating.

Day 264

Get Tech

If you don't remember any other tech-related recommendation from this book, I hope you will remember this one. Go to your computer and bookmark Richard Byrne's site, Free Tech for Teachers (www.freetech4teachers.com). The site was launched in 2007 and remains one of the most visited teacher blogs on the internet. Byrne has left almost no topic untouched; he has featured everything from ideas for assistive technology, to tips for UDL, to recommendations for motivating reluctant readers. Scroll down his page for a minute or two and you are sure to find a handful of ideas to use immediately in your school or classroom.

Share The News

If you want content appropriate for every reader in your classroom, you no longer need to gather a cartful materials for every single topic you teach. Simply click over to Newsela (www.newsela.com) and the work will be done for you. When you are teaching current events, working with informational text, or looking for ways to make daily lessons fresher and more relevant, you can access this site full of short news articles from a wide variety of publications including *The Philadelphia Inquirer*, *The Los Angeles Times*, and *The Milwaukee Journal-Sentinel*.

With the click of a mouse, users can adjust the readability of popular news articles. Students can choose from five different reading levels and can even make different choices for different articles as they browse. Therefore, if they have more interest in a certain topic than their peers and are, therefore, willing to power through a challenging article on it, they can opt to do so.

Teachers can search for articles by topics, grade level, and learning standards. Language is yet another choice educators and students can make as articles are available in both English and Spanish.

Make Math Accessible

Need help meeting all student needs in math lessons? Check out the Addressing Accessibility in Mathematics website (www2.edc.org/accessMath/resources/strategies.asp) for a variety of strategies and tools. Here, you will find lists of teaching ideas, formats for planning, links to research and more. And if you like that site, skip over to Math is Fun (www.mathsisfun.com) and check out the many resources offered there including a visual dictionary of terms and a variety of puzzles and games.

Predict Writing Success

As soon as your students are writing anything longer than a few sentences, some of them may need a word predication program. Co:writer (donjohnston.com/cowriter) is one of the very best tools of its kind, especially for learners needing a lot of support.

This product predicts which word a writer is attempting, and has millions of topic-specific dictionaries (e.g., *Julie of the Wolves*, heredity, Frederick Douglass). So, if a student is writing about measurement, Co:writer offers words like *unit*, *length*, *area*, *volume*, and *approximate*.

Also, after users have written a sentence, Co:writer can read the text back, so students can immediately assess their work and address any mistakes they may have overlooked.

Day 268

Start A Dialogue

You probably know Edmodo (www.edmodo.com) as "Facebook for school." With Edmodo, teachers can truly bring the classroom online. You can give assignments and quizzes, provide links and materials to support in-class learning, and, of course, involve students in discussions. You can also use Edmodo to support in-class book clubs, to assess student grammar and punctuation, to observe and assess discussions in foreign languages, and to investigate big questions (e.g., "What is my responsibility to the environment?" during a unit, semester, or year.

A program like Edmodo also allows for different types of interactions with students. Some who struggle to share in class may be quite outgoing in online conversations, and more serious students may show a lighter side when they are outside the classroom.

Find A Good Book

If you are looking for new ways to help students find books that match their interests and reading levels, check out Goodreads (www. goodreads.com). Students can add the teacher as a friend on the site and share book reviews, favorite topics and titles, and their reading progress.

This insight into reading behavior can be fruitful. You can find out about the unique interests of your students. You can learn about trends in their reading. You can also get useful information from the reviews students post including clues to their text comprehension. This, in turn, will help you make recommendations to your readers and plan your lessons.

Get Lit For All

Do you have a middle or high school student who is an emerging reader? If so, resist using primary books or pre-school activities. These types of teaching tools may embarrass the learner and, therefore, may impact his or her motivation.

To engage struggling readers in the upper grades, try magazines, coffee table books (with pictures and few words), or comics. You can also explore high-interest, low-level literacy materials from the following publishers:

> www.bearportpublishing.com

> www.highnoonbooks.com

> hip-books.com

> www.orcabook.com

> www.townsendpress.com

Share The Slant Board

If you have students with significant or multiple disabilities, they may need assistive technology to support their learning. While some of these tools are expensive and made available to only a few students in the school, others are fairly inexpensive and can be offered to a larger number of students, including those without identified needs. Invest in slant boards and desktop easels, hand-held magnifiers, pencils or pens adapted in size or grip diameter, alternative keyboards, and single-message communication devices for use in your UDL classroom.

Come On Down!

Do you want to have a little fun in the classroom today? Let your students compete and collaborate using game-show style apps as study supports.

There are many different tools that can be used to set up friendly classroom battles. Most of them allow users to access published quizzes and modify them for their own use. Most also offer results in a spreadsheet format, thus providing a snapshot of student learning and participation.

Ready to get started? Check out the following platforms:

› www.getkahoot.com

› www.socrative.com

› www.quizalize.com

› www.triventy.com.

Day 273

Connect In The Comments

If you have a classroom blog, you can use both the blog posts and the comments that follow as a way to teach and assess student writing and respectful discourse. Direct students to create posts that invite discussion and then support them as they both respond to and add comments. By focusing on this aspect of blogging, you can teach students to provide meaningful feedback, to build on the thoughts of others, and to encourage discussion and idea sharing.

Students who are skilled writers can be challenged to create detailed responses. Ask them to question, to muse, to elaborate on thoughts, and to engage with the post's author and others who comment. Other students with emerging skills in this area might share briefer comments, post images, or paste memes to communicate their thoughts and ideas.

Cross To New Classrooms

Use technology to connect to other classrooms. While you may have learners with many different viewpoints and backgrounds in your own classroom, connecting with those in other rooms, cities, states, and countries will provide you and your students with opportunities to widen your horizons even further.

You can choose any number of tools for this purpose, including Twitter (share a hashtag), Edmodo, or a shared blog.

There is an endless amount of potential here. Start with a Q & A session to teach one another about your respective schools or cities. Expand to a shared service project. Move on to a cross-classroom book study.

Capture It

Video recording is an effective and efficient way to capture learning over time. Recording can be used to track student progress, or illustrate mastery of a skill or learning standard for families, other teachers, or for students themselves. Video assessment may be especially helpful for students who have significant disabilities and may, therefore, demonstrate progress at a slower rate than their peers.

For example, a student with multiple disabilities participating in a kindergarten morning meeting may show very little evidence of participation in the first few weeks of school. Gradually, he or she may be able to show evidence of engagement (e.g., looking at the teacher). Eventually, he or she may be able to raise a hand, vocalize during a song, or answer a question using sign language. It might be hard to appreciate this learner's impressive progress if only traditional kindergarten assessment tools (e.g., observation, work samples) were used, but someone watching regularly captured video clips would likely notice the individual's growing ability.

Determine how you might use video assessment. Consider using this tool to evaluate

> study habits (e.g., working independently),

> social skills (e.g., taking turns),

> group work (e.g., sharing materials),

> literacy (e.g., reading fluently),

> communication (e.g., staying on topic),

> presentations (e.g., using appropriate voice volume),

> physical education (e.g., using equipment properly), and

> music (e.g., performing a piece of music).

Day
276

Share Images Instantly

Instagram (www.instagram.com) is a photo editing and social networking website. It is easy to use in the classroom because many students are already familiar with it and can coach their peers who haven't yet tried it.

Use Instagram to

> collect pictures related to a classroom topic;

> take pictures related to a classroom topic;

> make accounts for a particular book character or historical figure;

> have students post recommendations (e.g., books, content-focused movies);

> gather inspiration photos for art, research, or writing projects;

> invite students to a content-related picture-a-day challenge (e.g., pictures of living things, pictures of geometry in the world); and

> let students be photojournalists for a unit of study or experience.

Teachers can also use Instagram to share photos with students. So, learners can see images of the teacher's recommendations, favorite learning hacks, or writing project inspirations.

Say It With Sticky Notes

Sticky notes come in so many sizes and shapes, and are such a handy, low-tech support for UDL classrooms. You can jot letters or words on sticky notes and have students compose sentences without using a pencil, create a colorful word bank for a worksheet or test, or make a desktop reminder for a learner needing cues about how to solve problems or edit work.

Sticky notes can also be used

> as exit slips or response "cards,"

> as part of a mind map,

> to annotate text,

> to signal understanding to the teacher (e.g., green sticky on desk for "I understand" and red sticky for "I still have questions"),

> to share brainstorming ideas on the dry erase board,

> to flag passages in a novel or textbook,

> to create a collaborative line graph,

> to create a large-scale mural or mosaic,

> as an impromptu reading reflection,

> to communicate different directions/cues to different students in the classroom, or

> to add notes/ideas/illustrations to interactive notebooks.

You can also share, communicate, and connect electronically with sticky-note-inspired sites and apps. Try Padlet (www.padlet.com), Popplet (www.popplet.com), or GroupZap (groupzap.com) to organize information and create useful visual supports.

Go To The Movies

Use popular films to illustrate ideas and concepts across subject areas. This practice is motivating for learners and often gets them "studying" on their own time beyond the assignment.

In social studies, you might use *Apollo 13* when teaching about the space program, *Glory* and *Lincoln* when studying the Civil War, or the pre-honeymoon scene in *It's a Wonderful Life* to illustrate the human aspect of the Wall Street Crash of 1929.

In science, you can watch films to share stories and historical moments. You might screen *Ms. Evers' Boys* when teaching about ethics and science, *The Cove* when studying pollution, or *Super Size Me* to start a conversation about nutrition. You can also use films to illustrate misconceptions (e.g., show a noisy *Star Wars* battle and point out that there should be no sound in space).

Math teachers might show parts of *The Imitation Game* and *A Beautiful Mind* to teach about problem solving and specifically, about persevering in problem solving. And students of all ages will love *Donald in Mathmagic Land*.

You can show some films in language arts classes to have students compare them to the texts they are reading. Have students first read the books and discuss how they would cast them, what pieces of dialogue are most critical, and so on. Then view the films and compare students' visions with the director's choices. Possible choices include *Grapes of Wrath*, *To Kill a Mockingbird*, *Holes*, *The Book Thief*, *The BFG*, *Hugo*, and *The Life of Pi*. Films can also be used to teach content in other ways. You might have students study archetype by watching a film like *The Princess Bride* or explore examples of symbolism by viewing *The Wizard of Oz*.

Day 279

Make Learning Pop

Kids of all ages love cartoons. Take advantage of that interest by tuning into BrainPop (www.brainpop.com) shorts to supplement your lectures, reinforce concepts, or kick off a new unit. You can access some videos for free and for a small fee, your school or district can access dozens of animated clips that can be used to teach health, mathematics, science, social studies, and more. Films are available on any number of topics including animal classification, carbon dating, Malcolm X, inequalities, and cubism.

Use this site to engage reluctant learners, to immerse students in content related to their own interests, and to encourage learning beyond classroom walls.

Day 280

Compose Collaboratively

Some learners may struggle to share even a few words or lines of text. Students with intellectual disabilities, those on the autism spectrum, and those with physical disabilities may find it challenging to type a story, response, or essay, but may be able to express themselves using a word or two, or by pointing at images.

Collaborative writing assignments can be powerful for these individuals. You might have students with and without disabilities collaborate on a book review or three-sentence story using Twitter, or participate in an online discussion thread. Some students can contribute just a few words, while others can add sentences and paragraphs.

Another idea for collaborative writing is to ask a student with a disability to select a series of photos to use as a basis for an essay. Peers without disabilities can then add captions or fill in a story around the images.

Learning Environment

Change It Up With Groupings

There are limitless ways to group your students for instruction. You can group students with similar skills, interests, preferences, or needs, or you can put students with complementary abilities or talents together. You can also group them randomly to see how different students work together, and to build community in the classroom.

You will notice that some groupings will help students get support from peers, others will help them share their interests, learn new roles, make social connections, or hone their leadership skills. Questions you might want to use to balance group roles, needs, and abilities include:

> - Do these groups have at least one natural leader or facilitator?

> - Do these groups have at least one person who regularly takes on a support role and will help those who need it?

> - Do these groups have at least one member with expertise, knowledge, or skill in the target topic?

> - Do these groups have at least one enthusiastic member who will encourage others?

> - Do these groups have at least one student with strong organization skills?

> - Do these groups have a mix of students with different challenges and strengths?

> - Does every student have a friend (or preferred work partner) in his or her group?

Day 282

Stock Their Boxes

Give every student in your classroom a mailbox or bin so you can stock it with materials, reading recommendations, notes, and missing work. This sort of direct communication will allow you to channel materials to students even when they are not with you, and differentiate the products that you provide to them. On any given day, you might provide some students with short articles related to their interests, others with new magazines to peruse, and still others with new notepads to fill with thoughts and reflections.

Add Some Art

Today, transform your classroom into an art studio. During a discussion or mini-lecture, let students illustrate ideas on paper-covered tables or on huge rolls of paper. Have them create oversized maps. Give them large canvases to create large-scale illustrations related to the stories or novels you are studying. Encourage them to take visual notes using paint, grease pencils, or thick markers. Distribute blank books and let students rewrite a segment of the textbook using drawings, sketches, and different colors and fonts.

Post their creations on the walls and tables of your classroom.

Get Out

Do your students need a boost? Try a shift in the learning environment. This simple change may literally awaken some of your students. Go outside to read and write short stories. Sketch neighboring buildings on a walk around the block. Go out to the playground and tape off a variety of polygons. Study state wildflowers in a neighboring field. Explore community resources. Take a run up the street. Photograph graffiti. Draw diagrams on the concrete using sidewalk chalk. Skip count while you skip across the school's front lawn. Speak Spanish, German, or Japanese while walking around the neighborhood and making observations.

Learning Environment

Push Those Pedals

Movement is so important for students of all ages. Emphasize this by giving as many opportunities as possible for students to move as they learn. This recommendation may not be possible for every teacher, but some may be able to install an exercise bike (or even two) in the classroom that can be used as a learning station ("Ride & Read"), a brain break for individual learners, or a rotating support for any learner needing an energy boost.

Set Up An Oasis

Convert some classroom or building space into a quiet study area that any student can access when needed. Your oasis might consist of a chair in the back of a classroom, a study carrel in a school library, or a small repurposed conference room. Offer the space to any student who needs a break from the commotion of the classroom.

The oasis can be used for five- or ten-minute breaks, or it can be utilized as a quiet study area for one or two students who occasionally need to work without distractions.

Take Time For Teambuilding

Use cooperative games, active learning structures, and community-building activities to encourage students to get and give support and learn from one another. Teambuilding helps students feel more confident in their learning. It can also make the classroom feel safer and more comfortable for your diverse learners.

Use the following ideas to grow your classroom community, strengthen student connections, and build teaming skills:

> Read books about collaboration.

> Play "getting to know you" games.

> Hold classroom meetings to resolve conflicts, plan events, and reflect on learning.

> Let students teach mini-lessons about their interests, passions, and areas of expertise.

> Ask students to write stories and essays expressing their thoughts, ideas, and values; share these with the class.

> Create art (e.g., a chalk mural, a mosaic) as a group.

You might also ask students for ideas on teambuilding.

Make Smart Matches

In a UDL classroom, groupings change throughout the day and year so that students have opportunities to work with all classmates and learn from each one of them on a regular basis. Some teachers regularly allow learners to choose partners or team members. Although this practice gives students opportunities to work with familiar peers, it can also cause isolation and frustration in the classroom for those who are not asked to be a partner or team member. Furthermore, students who choose partners and team members for every activity may constantly select from the same peer group. When this happens, students fail to become acquainted with and learn from all class members, and the community of the classroom is threatened.

One way to honor preferences while engineering groupings that benefit all learners is to ask students to give input on group formation. Teachers might ask students to provide this information informally through a short interview or by listing a few names on a sheet of paper, or they might be asked to fill out a worksheet that provides more detailed information about grouping preferences. Of course, this tool should be used to give students opportunities to learn about their learning, so instead of inviting them to list those that they want in their group, ask for the names of "a few students with whom you feel you can do your best work."

Play It Again

Allow students with sensory challenges to use headphones to listen to soft music in noisy or chaotic environments. In some situations, you may also want to play calming music for all learners. Explore this option specifically with learners who seem in need of a break, or those who appear overwhelmed by the daily bustle of the classroom.

See The Light

The right lighting can soothe, calm, energize, or inspire students. Alternatively, the wrong lighting can be annoying and distracting.

Florescent lighting in particular can impact learning, behavior, and the comfort level of some students with autism and learning disabilities. In order to determine whether florescent lights are problematic for your students, limit the use of the overhead lights for a day to see if the change seems to make a difference. If the lighting does seem to be a concern, experiment with different ways of brightening your classroom:

> Try lower levels of light for lessons, when appropriate.

> Take advantage of natural light. Sit your student with sensory problems close to the windows.

> Use upward-projecting rather than downward-projecting lighting, when possible.

> Experiment with different types of lighting. Turn on the front bank of lights, but not the back or turn on alternating banks of lights, for instance.

> Suggest sunglasses or a baseball cap to help sensitive students avoid direct exposure to light.

Cozy Up

A sure way to help students succeed in your classroom is to create a pleasant work space. You might create a more comfortable classroom by investing in an area rug, or by putting an armchair in a corner. If you can, paint the walls a soothing color. Make sure materials are neatly stored. Keep learning spaces tidy.

For the best possible results, ask your students for input on designing the ideal classroom. Implement any ideas that are reasonable and that might allow a wider range of students to feel comfortable and work productively.

Drink Up

Ask students to bring water bottles to school and encourage them to take sips throughout the day. Drinking water will help them concentrate every day, but this practice will be especially helpful during stressful times (e.g., first day of school, testing week).

Be sure to consult with families or your school nurse about those who have specific needs related to hydration due to certain disabilities, health conditions, or medications.

Day 293

Give Them The Floor

Don't have funds for seating supports? Use what you do have!

You might, for instance, offer students the choice of sitting at their desks or on the floor. Those choosing to sit on the floor can work on clipboards or use lap desks. You might also provide them with reading pillows or inexpensive seat cushions to make their work space more comfortable.

Standing is another freebie seating option. Some students may want to stay on their feet for all or part of a lesson. If you don't have standing desks in your classroom for these students, try offering a lectern as a writing surface.

Create Rituals

Create daily and weekly rituals that will honor those who seek consistency, help students meet learning goals, and build a sense of togetherness in the classroom. A fifth-grade teacher might plan collaborative review games on Friday afternoons. A band teacher might use part of her Monday classes for informal jam sessions. An English teacher might host 10-minute spoken word slams on Tuesdays.

Rituals are not only soothing to a great many students, but they allow educators to keep some part of their schedule consistent which can make planning a bit easier, especially when it involves a partner or a small team.

Make Arrangements

Make UDL lessons easy to implement by getting your learning space ready for movement and impromptu rearranging. Set your desks in clusters to make collaboration easier. Show students how to move furniture to support partner and individual work. Provide portable worktables that can be moved to any area of the classroom. Offer easels, when possible, so some learners can stand and take notes. Have a bin of clipboards available for groups who might need to sit on the floor or for those who may need to work in an area without a table or desk.

Take A Walk

Why not take a triangle, compound word, autumn, primary color, living thing, visual metaphor, or pop art walk today? Have students stroll around the building, playground, or neighborhood, and jot down or photograph examples of the concept you are studying.

Some topics lend themselves to this strategy better than others, of course, but if you are creative, you will find many possible applications. For example, you don't need to use the walk only for things that can be seen or observed; you can also use it for inspiration. If you want students to compose a piece of music, have them walk for 15 minutes and write about something they see, feel, or experience.

Promote Healthy Learning

So often, we focus all of our energy on curriculum and instruction without considering how else we can meet the needs of students. Today, consider how you might support students by creating a healthier classroom. Think about one change you could make to help one, some, or all students feel more alert, stay energetic, and work comfortably. Could you remind students to hydrate more often? Give them time to have a healthy snack? Provide healthy snacks? Give opportunities for movement or even light exercise through brain breaks or collaborative activities?

There may even be classroom norms you want to examine. For instance, giving out candy as a reward for correct answers may seem like a good way to motivate the class, but what this practice actually does is heighten the desire for sugar, interfere with natural hunger cues, and, potentially worst of all, teach students to use food as a reward. In other words, it's really unhealthy. It will also do nothing to increase the attention and liveliness of your students and may, in fact, zap their energy.

 **Relax!**

Stress and anxiety are horrible states for learning. Therefore, if you want students to thrive in your classroom, introduce calming techniques that they can use throughout the school day and beyond. Consider

> playing soothing music at certain times,

> introducing guided meditation or relaxation exercises,

> teaching deep breathing,

> allowing short walking breaks, and

> using low lighting for certain lessons.

As you become more aware of calming tools and more savvy at integrating them into the day, you may be able to personalize options for students. Every learner need not take daily meditation breaks, but some may need a stack of cue cards for this purpose, and a few students may need a little time to chill out with soft music on a regular basis.

Use That Tune

Use music in transitions or as a cue for certain behaviors or activities (e.g., play quiz show music while students are brainstorming in small groups). Music can expand the experiences of learners and change the energy of the classroom. It can also be used as part of the curriculum. For instance, you can play "We Shall Overcome" when teaching the U.S. Civil Rights Movement or "Hound Dog" to teach metaphors.

Let Them Fidget

If you are teaching a lesson that will last longer than 15 minutes, some learners may need a fidget toy or sensory object to keep their hands occupied. Some students may only need an occasional desktop tool, and others may need a whole collection of materials to remain calm, on task, and focused. Talk to your school's occupational therapist to get ideas about supports that will work well with students with identified needs, or simply offer a range of toys and gadgets until you find good matches for particular learners. Common classroom fidgets include

> bumpy or spiny balls/gel bead balls,

> squeeze or tangle toys,

> kneadable erasers,

> finger puzzles,

> bean bags, and

> foot bands.

If you find you have a whole host of students who need sensory support, consider a DIY approach to stocking your fidget bag. When you make your own or use common classroom materials as fidgets, you can not only customize your materials for individual learners, but you can also offer options to all students in your classroom and not just those with disabilities or identified sensory needs. Ideas for homemade or inexpensive store-bought fidgets include

> sand-filled balloon stress balls,

> play dough,

> coiled keychains,

> pool noodle rings/slices,

> interesting pencil toppers, and

> slinky toys.

Check The Time

Use a timer as a visual or auditory reminder to keep students on task.

Once you incorporate a timer for some tasks (e.g., project-based instruction, centers, warm-up exercises) students are often more relaxed and focused. A student who is constantly worrying or asking others, "How much time is left?" is often distracted and unnecessarily attending to everything but the task at hand.

Other functions for a classroom timer include

› helping students learn time management,

› keeping the teacher on task,

› minimizing unnecessary verbal instructions,

› communicating with students without interrupting their work, and

› engineering and managing varied activities.

You may also want to use timers with individual students. In these situations, provide handheld kitchen timers, or apps on cellphones or tablets.

Learning Environment

Go To The Library

Set up all your students for literacy success. Make sure all learners have appropriate materials and that your classroom is as literacy-rich as possible.

Classroom libraries should contain at least 600 to 1,500 titles (Allington, 2011). School libraries should be open and accessible to all students for more than a few hours a week. Students should get to choose what they read whenever possible. At all grade levels, both teachers and students should recommend selections to one another. All of these practices ensure that students get what they need for literacy success, and that they have a range of ways to access reading materials, to interact with other readers, and to learn from books and other print materials.

 **Day**

Profile Them

At the beginning of the year, have students create a profile card. They should describe their learning preferences, a few of their interests, and some of their strengths. Younger students will need boxes to check or pictures to circle. Older students may simply need to see a few examples in order to successfully complete the task.

Use these cards to get to know students, to plan lessons, and to make learning relevant. You can also use profile cards to assemble groups.

Keep It Up During Down Time

Make the most of the day by occasionally using the moments before school, after school, and passing time as opportunities to learn. Spell out group or table names when you give directions (e.g., "Line up if you are sitting at the a-l-l-i-g-a-t-o-r table"). As students filter into your classroom, play intriguing news clips or You Tube videos. Engage in two-minute conferences with students who arrive to the classroom a bit on the early side.

Get Help

Have you ever needed to call a help desk for assistance? If so, you probably found relief from your problem on the other end of the line. Wouldn't it be nice to create that kind of help desk experience in the classroom?

Your help desk might include a laptop or two (especially critical if students do not have their own devices), some reference books, literature related to current lessons, a list/binder of student names and their corresponding interests and areas of expertise, and supplies that might be useful or needed by some or all learners (e.g., LiveScribe pen, highlighter, large-button calculator). Virtual supports might include teacher-created outlines/notes, helpful videos, work product examples, and links to study and learning tips.

 **Day 306**

Shush!

Background noise can affect every student's ability to learn, but it can be especially troublesome for those who are Deaf or hard of hearing. Evaluate the room to determine if noises from computers, heating and cooling systems, or the shuffling of furniture and supplies can be minimized or eliminated. If the screech of moving desks and seats is problematic, for instance, tennis balls can be attached to the feet of tables and chairs to eliminate the offending sound.

Materials

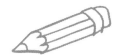

DIY Your School Supplies

When a student presents a unique learning challenge, it may be necessary to head to the teacher store or Amazon.com to find the tools needed to respond to that challenge. Before you do so, however, be sure to look around the classroom, comb through your closet, and survey your supplies. Learning materials don't always have to be replaced or added in these situations; sometimes you may simply need to adapt or repurpose what you already have. Slide a few bolts down the shaft of a pencil and secure it with a rubber band to create a weighted pencil. Push a paint brush through a tennis ball to create an artist's tool that is easier to grip. Turn a five-inch binder on its side and use it as a slant board. Use an ironing board as a standing desk. Assemble PVC pipes to make a book stand.

Draw A Blank

Blank books—either those purchased at discount stores or student-created versions—are necessities in UDL classrooms. You can use them for hundreds of purposes at every single grade level.

Let students use blank books for

- › creating one-sentence daily diaries,
- › writing short autobiographies,
- › nature sketching,
- › goal setting,
- › recording favorite quotes,

- › making a magazine,
- › writing a sequel to a favorite book,
- › starting an art journal,
- › illustrating vocabulary words, or
- › collaborative journaling.

Introduce blank books of all sizes. Keep in mind, however, that students with motor problems may want to use larger books or books with lined pages.

Dot It

Get a package of brightly colored dot stickers. This inexpensive teaching tool can be used to

> group students quickly and easily (e.g., put them in teams with students with same or different colored dots),

> help with classroom management (e.g., put stickers on desks, those with "greens" should distribute papers),

> liven up a math lesson (e.g., use dots as sticky "manipulatives"),

> inspire the creation of unique images (e.g., fission vs. fusion diagram, story problem pictures), and

> code books in your classroom library (e.g., orange means "the teacher recommends"; pink means "quick read").

Go To The Box

Add some fun and game-show-style intrigue to the classroom by creating an inspiration box. It's easy to make and even easier to integrate into your daily or weekly routine. Empty out a cube-shaped tissue box, cover it with paper or duct tape, and fill it with index cards.

Draw a card daily or weekly to provide students with

> a challenge (e.g., "Teach your family how to mediate"),

> a tip (e.g., "Hydrate when you study; water will give you energy"), or

> a recommendation (e.g., "Read a poem by Langston Hughes you have never read before").

Stock the box yourself or let students add items.

 **Teach With Fluffy**

Bring a basketful of plush animals into the classroom and use them to create unique and memorable learning experiences. Not only will a crate of kittens or bag of birds inspire laughter, it can also provide a little motivation and add some fun to your lesson.

Younger students can use plush toys as reading partners. They can read to their buddies or just cuddle them as they enjoy a good book. They can also use their toys as students; teach a concept or skill to students and have them turn around and teach it to their stuffed pals. In the upper grades, use toys as response objects; throw the animal to students to elicit responses during a class discussion.

You can also use stuffed toys as

> classroom mascots,

> writing prompts (e.g., "Create a story using this animal or creature as a main character"), or

> turn-taking tools (e.g., only the person holding the toy can talk/respond/participate).

Day 312

Tap, Tap, Tap

Illuminate learning by investing in a few tap lights. These lights are usually purchased to brighten up a closet or attic, but you can use them to "shine up" a lesson or two.

Use your tap lights as a sensory support. Shut off the overhead lights for part of the day and substitute with these portable options when students are listening or engaged in discussions and don't need to view materials.

You can also use your tap light as a communication tool. As students work in groups to answer questions or create products, have them tap their lights to indicate they are ready to respond or show their work.

How about using your lights to create dynamic visuals? Design a solar system model and "light up" every plant. Draw the parts of a cell on the dome and create a memorable model.

Finally, consider using tap lights in a classroom competition. If you play group review games like Taboo, Jeopardy, or trivia, use tap lights to have students "ring in" their answers. The first to illuminate the tap light gets to answer.

Offer A Greeting

Use greeting cards as a novel way to get students writing. Look for blank cards with captivating, funny, or poignant photos. Pass one to each student and ask him or her to write a short story, poem, or essay based on the image they have been assigned. To make this activity less abstract and easier for some to complete, add a word bank, story starter, or even cloze paragraphs to the inside covers of certain cards.

Don't have enough greeting cards for everyone in the class? Fill in the gap with postcards, brochures, magazine pictures, or trading cards.

If you want to use this activity on a regular basis, ask families to contribute materials.

Pre-Cut The Paper

Some students with physical disabilities, autism, and sensory needs cannot easily cut, draw, or color. For these learners, it is important to provide a collection of supplies to encourage participation. Some examples are

> adapted scissors,

> stencils,

> pencil grips,

> slant boards/easels,

> stamps/stickers,

> photographs/magazine pictures,

> pre-cut paper shapes,

> work trays (to keep paper and materials in place),

> "rock" or extra-large crayons,

> easy-grip paint brushes,

> alternative paint brushes (e.g., sponges, rolling pins),

> dab/BINGO markers,

> finger paint,

> paint pens, and

> drawing/painting/design software or apps.

Keep in mind that these materials may be needed for some students, but preferred by others. If one or two artists are accessing these materials, why not let others try them too?

Day 315

Make It Stick

Stickers are an effective and inexpensive support for students who have fine motor problems, or for those who need a bit of motivation or inspiration. They can also be a helpful shortcut for those who are working on a fill-in-the-blank worksheet, creating drawings, engaging in classroom exercises, or journaling, and they offer a more tactile alternative to software programs that provide a similar sort of support.

Stickers can be used across grade levels. For example, a first-grade student who is working on a math sheet can use both picture and number stickers to create his or her own story problems. A fourth-grade student who needs to label a map of the Great Lakes can do so by affixing a pre-printed sticker to each body of water. And an eighth-grade student who is creating a haiku with a partner can peel and stick word or phrase stickers to build the perfect poem.

Don't have the stickers you need for an activity? Make your own by printing images on labels and cutting to size.

Day 316

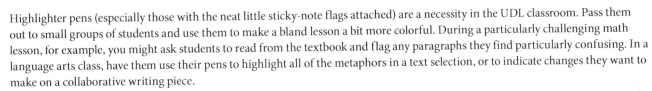

Flag It

Highlighter pens (especially those with the neat little sticky-note flags attached) are a necessity in the UDL classroom. Pass them out to small groups of students and use them to make a bland lesson a bit more colorful. During a particularly challenging math lesson, for example, you might ask students to read from the textbook and flag any paragraphs they find particularly confusing. In a language arts class, have them use their pens to highlight all of the metaphors in a text selection, or to indicate changes they want to make on a collaborative writing piece.

Think Beyond The Tablet

To keep all students interested in writing, introduce a wide range of materials. Most students today are offered the use of tablets as an alternative to pencil and paper, but keep in mind that some students will want a little more variety to keep them inspired and productive. For these individuals, you might occasionally offer colored pencils, drawing software programs, sensory art supplies (e.g., shaving cream, silly string), letter or word stickers, label makers, and/or magnetic words and phrases.

And keep this recommendation in mind beyond the language arts classroom. How about offering pencils, pens, markers, stamps, stickers, or even paint to first graders who are working on math facts? How about letting high school students choose to complete a geometry assignment with pencils, chalk, or iPads?

Keep exploring new writing tools throughout the year to see which ones inspire your students the most.

Fold 'Em Up

Foldables™ are three-dimensional projects that serve as interactive graphic organizers. Students learn from creating the resource, and from using it as a reference during classroom activities.

Popularized by Dinah Zike (1992), Foldables™ are very popular with teachers in K–12 classrooms. Educators use them to teach any number of concepts, including cause and effect, point of view, pro/con debates, story elements, timelines, vocabulary, and main ideas. There are many types of Foldables™ that can be used to teach these concepts. A 4-flap (folding a paper in half and cutting the front of the paper into four sections so that each section can be lifted to see the paper underneath), for instance, can be created to teach the life cycle of a frog. On the front flaps, students create a label and/or an image for that piece of the content then lift to see a detailed description or definition. So, the life cycle of a frog Foldable™ would feature eggs on the first flap, a tadpole on the second, and so on.

You can easily make Foldable™ activities work in a UDL classroom. First, you can have some students embellish their creations and make them more detailed. You can also provide partially assembled products for students needing more support. For instance, you might provide the text in the form of a large sticker, and allow students to add their own illustrations. Or you might create both the text and the illustrations and give students the task of underlining key words and phrases, or adding details with stamps or highlighters.

Day
319

Tape It Off

Don't even think about setting up your UDL classroom without a roll of duct tape or two or three or more. Gather a few different patterns and styles and affix away.

Use tape to

> stick visual cues to your walls or floor (e.g., grids, music staff, diagrams),

> color code school supplies for a learner with organization struggles,

> create work space on a side of a file cabinet or table (mask off a magnetic work area with tape or cover it all with chalkboard or dry erase tape),

> decorate shelves or boxes for different purposes (e.g., blue box for challenge work, red box for practice work), or

> separate your dry erase board into segments to organize content, reminders, and information.

Day
320

Add An Image

Some students may need to use symbols, pictures, and illustrations to replace or supplement their written work. For example, a student with multiple disabilities may create a photo essay of flying insects in lieu of a paper on them. A learner with Down syndrome may want to write a fable using words, phrases, and a few Google Image photos.

Let learners with expression and communication struggles use images to

> answer specific questions,

> assemble more detailed lab notes,

> embellish journal entries,

> compose stories and essays, and

> create unique art work.

Day 321

Find A Replacement

Some students will need replacement materials for certain lessons because those provided are somehow inappropriate for them. For instance, a kindergarten student who cannot easily illustrate his daily writing journal may need to use stickers and stamps or a drawing app on a tablet instead of crayons and colored pencils. Some middle school students may need graph paper instead of notebook pages so they can keep rows and columns of numbers straight when solving problems. A student with cerebral palsy may have fine and gross motor challenges, and, therefore, may require more durable materials in the science lab, such as beakers made of plastic instead of glass.

Assign Tasks

The next time you assign problems from the textbook or a worksheet, ask, "Could I use task cards for this lesson instead?"

Task cards are a motivating alternative to desktop work because they fracture the content into small pieces and give students opportunities to tackle assignments one item at a time.

Task cards can be used in many different ways. You can create task card stations where learners are assigned to complete certain activities in a short period of time. You can use them as enrichment or extension choices. They can be incorporated into partner or small group games. Or, you can assign them daily or weekly for practice on a skill that is a challenge for your learners (e.g., solving story problems).

Task cards are a useful tool in the UDL classroom. Struggling students can complete cards with multiple choice or fill-in-the-blank answers if open-ended problems are too challenging. Another option is to allow variety in how students respond; some can write answers and others can share responses verbally.

Day 323

Show The Work

Dry erase boards should be a staple in the UDL classroom. Most commonly they are used as a whole-class response tool. Each student has a board and the entire class responds to a prompt or question at the same time. Students can use their boards to

> solve math problems,

> illustrate words/concepts,

> create "Top 10" lists,

> answer questions,

> make "doodle notes,"

> draw diagrams, or

> create graphic organizers.

When using dry erase boards, you can ask all students to answer in the same way, or you might allow learners to respond in any way they choose (e.g., "Draw or write a definition for *hierarchy*").

Don't have enough dry erase boards for all of your students? Don't worry! Plastic "paper" plates or old compact disc cases work almost as well and can be purchased for just a few dollars at discount stores.

Roll The Dice

Every teacher has a pair of dice or—more likely—several sets of them. So, gather them up and use them as tools for supporting any number of games or classroom activities.

Use them to

> roll for group roles (e.g., 1 = summarizer, 2 = illustrator),

> choose activities or assessments (e.g., 1 = define the word, 2 = use the word in a sentence),

> pick which item/s on a worksheet to complete (e.g., shake one die and complete the problem corresponding to that number, shake two dice and do the same),

> select words/ideas from a numbered list to incorporate into a story, or

> randomly sort students into groups (e.g., Talia = group 6, Willow = group 2).

You can, of course, make your own dice if you don't have any or if you want to move beyond dots and numbers. You can buy blank cubes from teacher stores and websites or you can make your own by covering tissue boxes or drawing on blocks or foam cubes. Your DIY dice can then be filled with numbers, words, phrases, problems, or questions.

 **Day 325**

Cook Up Some Support

Cookbook stands are great low-tech supports for students with motor problems or physical disabilities. You can use them to prop up textbooks, papers, and artwork for those who struggle to grasp or hold materials. You can also use them as stands for tablets.

Cookbook stands can also be used to highlight items in your classroom. Use one to prop up a book recommendation related to current course content, a dry erase board that features a "fact of the day", or a sign featuring directions for a learning station.

Play Poker

Poker chips are an around-the-house item that you can bring into the classroom to motivate students and vary learning experiences.

Use them to track participation in a group discussion. Give every student a different color and tell them to place a poker chip on the table each time they contribute to the conversation. This allows both the students and the teacher to keep track of who is participating and who may need encouragement to do so.

Chips can also be used as manipulatives in the math classroom; students can make sets and subsets, story problems, arrays, or bar graphs with them.

How about putting your poker chips to work as a flexible grouping tool? Use them to form pairs, trios, and small groups (e.g., "Find two other people with chips that are the same color as your chip").

Finally, you can use these versatile game pieces to make "challenge chips"; just affix a question sticker to each disc and give students opportunities to draw one from a pouch when their work is completed.

Read Your Roles

Make instruction available to all by assigning certain students unique roles during cooperative games, structures, or group work. For example, if most students are engaged in small group discussions, one or two might serve as facilitators. Another might be asked to function as a note taker or recorder. These roles can be appointed based either on the strengths or the needs of your students.

To make role assignments easier for students to remember, consider making cards that highlight responsibilities for various roles. A note taking card, for instance, could list the following tasks:

> listen to the group discussion;

> record key points and ideas; and

> read the notes at the end of the lesson and ask group members for input.

Shuffle Them

To shuffle students in a unique way, use a deck of cards as a tool to form pairs, trios, and other groups.

Give each learner a card. When you are ready to form groups, give a direction related to the cards. You can do this randomly, or pre-plan the groups, depending on the goal of the activity. Possible directions include

> "Get into a group of four, making sure all four suits are represented",

> "Get into a group of four with others holding cards of the same suit",

> "Get into a group of three with two others who have the same color card you have",

> "Find a partner who shares your number or face card",

> "Find a partner who is holding a card of a different color", and

> "Find a partner who is holding a card of a different suit.

You can also use your decks of cards for other classroom purposes. Bring them out for math activities (e.g., playing multiplication "war"; making number sentences) or team-building games (e.g., card house competitions), for instance.

Teaching Strategies

Put Them To The Test

Adapting a test is very similar to adapting a worksheet or other written assignment. The most important elements to keep in mind are the student's reading level, expressive ability, targeted learning objectives, and physical needs or limitations (e.g., inability to read small print, difficulty holding a pencil). For example, if the student is in sixth grade but reads at a second-grade level and has mild intellectual disabilities, then simplified language and a modification of key concepts may be required. If a student has difficulty writing, paper-and-pencil assessments might be avoided altogether.

To adapt a test, you might

> allow students to dictate or record their answers;

> create less complex questions;

> take the test "off the page" and allow some answers to be performance-based (e.g., have students match flash cards instead of matching items on the test itself);

> allow students to use their own notes;

> allow the use of crib notes or a "cheat sheet";

> allow students to write all or some of the test questions;

> provide examples (with answers) of each type of question;

> add icons, pictures, or other visuals to help students understand the directions or the content;

> use highlighters to draw students' attention to the directions in each section;

> use an app like SnapType [SnapType] to move the test to a tablet and allow the student to type instead of write responses;

> enlarge the text or create an e-version so that students can adjust the readability themselves; or

> change the format of questions from short answer to fill-in-the-blank, multiple choice, or matching.

Make Magic

Use this quickie assessment trick when you have a few minutes at the end of the class period. Stand next to the door as students leave and have each one tell you a "magic word" before they go. Be sure that it is something short and simple (e.g., "Share a pronoun"; "Tell me how to say *dog* in Spanish"; "Name a type of polygon").

This process should be fun and light and should not be used to actually stop students from exiting, so if some of your "wordsmiths" are going to need help, be sure to give them a cue card or cheat sheet, pair them with a partner for support, or position them near the end of the line so they can eavesdrop a bit on other students.

Build On What Works

Stuck on how to support a certain student? Talk to his or her previous teachers. Ask about effective strategies and seek information about what the student does well.

Better yet, visit my website and download a tool I call "Strengths and Strategies" (www.paulakluth.com/readings/inclusive-schooling/strengths-and-strategies). This tool will prompt you to work with a group of individuals to gather ideas for support. The group you gather may include—but is not limited to—previous teachers, current teachers, therapists, family members, and peers. "Strengths and Strategies" can be used to problem-solve during a behavior meeting, design appealing learning experiences, or support a learner's transition from one grade level to the next.

Invite Participation

All students should be equipped to participate in classroom discussions. Therefore, if you have some who struggle to engage in a large-group setting, you may need to get a little creative. There are a variety of ways to engineer a student's participation during whole-class work. You might begin the discussion with a question the learner knows well, or plant a question or comment on an index card and give it to him or her to read at some point. You can also give this learner a unique role during interactive lectures, discussions, and presentations. Let him or her co-present pieces of the lesson or use their augmentative communication system to choose which examples, stories, or visuals are shared with the group.

Get Dressed Up

Want to motivate learners and make lessons memorable? Incorporate the occasional costume to drive your message home. How about dressing up like Edison to discuss inventions? Or like Clara Barton when teaching the Civil War? Or even as a desert or wetland when teaching habitats?

Work as part of a co-teaching team? Coordinate outfits to match your units. How about teaching as metaphor and simile; mitosis and meiosis; two suffragettes; or even slope and intercept?

Invite History

Bring lessons to life by inviting the community into the classroom. Teaching about 9/11? Have students invite their parents in to interview them about their memories. Learning about Pearl Harbor? Ask senior citizens to visit and share their recollections from December 7th, 1941. Studying a weather-related event like The Schoolhouse Blizzard or The Johnstown Flood? Ask a meteorologist from the local television station or college to come and give a mini-lecture on the topic.

This strategy allows students to explore events and experiences in a very personal way. It also allows those with particular interest in the targeted topics to know where to turn for additional information.

Throw In A Surprise

Use the element of surprise as a strategy for making lessons memorable. Adding novelty to the day is an effective way to provide support, engagement, and challenge. Surprise can be added in a number of ways. Come to school in a standards-based costume (e.g., atom, Frida Kahlo). Introduce a new game. Celebrate something. Play some music. Invite an interesting guest speaker. Let students take over for part of the day. Sing. Let them dance. Try some improv. Teach outside. Integrate unusual objects (e.g., hula hoops, puppets) into your lessons. Let them chat. Use sound effects. Present them with a group puzzle or mystery to solve. Hide something in the room. Bring in some musical instruments. Have an impromptu read-a-thon, joke fest, or talent show.

Summarize Succinctly

There are so many ways to summarize. Think creatively in order to inspire students. You can have them

> create an content-related analogy,

> write a tabloid-type headline that cleverly communicates the concept currently being discussed,

> create an acrostic of summary phrases using a word related to learning,

> compose a series of faux text-messages related to the lesson,

> invent a tee-shirt slogan to illustrate a particular concept from lecture,

> write a sentence incorporating the who/what/when/where/why/how of the material, or

> paraphrase a piece of content for a specific audience (e.g., younger children; readers of the class blog).

Take A Break

Engage your learners by integrating brain breaks into daily instruction. A brain break is an energizing activity that lasts less than five minutes, but helps students wake up, focus, and have a little fun. Breaks can be connected to content, but don't necessarily have to be.

Examples of brain breaks include

> - jumping jacks,
> - toe touches,
> - Simon Says,
> - Rock-Paper-Scissors,
> - three-step-handshake,

> - charades,
> - beach ball toss,
> - hot potato,
> - YMCA dance,
> - conga line,

> - stretching,
> - one-song dance party,
> - air spelling or air drawing,
> - thumb wrestling,
> - arm circles,

> - freeze dancing, and
> - one-minute walk and talk.

To learn more about brain breaks in the classroom and to find many examples, visit Energizing Brain Breaks (www.brainbreaks. blogspot.com) and GoNoodle (www.gonoodle.com).

Prep Them

Some students struggle mightily when new assessment tools are introduced. These individuals may need support to be successful.

If possible, share the format (e.g., computer or paper/pencil) and question length and type (e.g., multiple choice) of new assessments with your students. In addition, let them know how long the assessment might take to complete.

You might also want to prepare your students for assessments by giving them choices about testing conditions and the environment. If possible, give them an option of where to sit, what materials to use (e.g., clipboard and pen or iPad), and which parts of the assessment to complete first.

Float With Purpose

As you move through the classroom to facilitate activities and provide feedback to students, do so with focus. For each lesson, consider how to best support learners and provide the richest learning experience possible. During some lessons, you may want to observe student behaviors (e.g., cooperation, listening, providing meaningful feedback, participation). During other lessons, you may focus primarily on giving feedback on the content (e.g., using a range of problem-solving strategies, developing a clear thesis).

To ensure you are "floating with purpose," you may want to use an assessment tool during some lessons. For instance, you might design a checklist to keep track of your observations. This will serve as a reminder of student conversations, and as a record of which students you observed or informally assessed, and which ones you have not yet seen.

Teach To The Rhythm

If you are a child of the 1970s, you may have learned about how a bill becomes a law by watching *School House Rocks* clips between Saturday morning cartoons. These videos made learning entertaining and memorable.

Why not bring this type of charm and humor into your own teaching? Make your content unforgettable by using strategies that focus on rhythm, patterns, and music.

Teach mnemonic devices (e.g., HOMES = Huron, Ontario, Michigan, Erie, and Superior). Introduce songs or raps to remember new vocabulary words. Cheer or chant math facts. Create jingles to kick off a new unit of study. Charge students with choreographing movements that illustrate new concepts.

Get Them Talking

So many students need interaction in order to learn and retain material. Many of these same students need daily practice to sharpen their communication and social skills. Therefore, opportunities for collaboration, connection, and chatting often benefit students in many ways. These opportunities also profit teachers; getting students to "think out loud" gives educators a chance to informally assess what is being taught and make adjustments as needed.

To get and keep them talking, you can use any number of response techniques. You might regularly move students into small groups so they can learn with and from one another. Or you can throw a response object (e.g., beach ball, stuffed toy) around the classroom to elicit quick responses from a variety of students. You might ask anyone who catches the toy to share one thing (e.g., one fact about the brain, a compound word). You can also play "stand and share" where you call out a category (e.g., March birthdays, wearing tennis shoes) and anyone fitting that category has to stand and provide a response.

Day
342

Show Off

Rubrics, guidelines, and detailed direction sheets can help students complete a multi-step assessment, but if you want them to create the best possible products, be sure to give them high-quality examples. If you want students to write detailed book reviews, have a handful available for students to peruse. Write your own or share links to Goodreads (www.goodreads.com) or Amazon (www.amazon.com). Showing students examples that do not make the grade can also be helpful.

To "show off" for your students, consider collecting samples of

- essays,
- geometric proofs,

- research papers,
- annotated bibliographies,

- lab notes, and
- portfolios.

Show & Tell

Some students may not be able to follow a lecture without related visual supports, and most others will be more engaged and interested if there are props, notes, diagrams, photos, models, or illustrations that support the content. By simply scanning lesson plans and asking, "How can I show, demonstrate, or illustrate this concept or lesson?", you may come up with fresh ideas you had not previously considered.

Use photographs to illustrate challenging vocabulary words like *indignant*, *nefarious*, and *vociferous*. Create infographics with tools like Pictochart (www.piktochart.com) and Venngage (www.venngage.com) and use them to share facts about the continents or eras in history. Make colorful posters of diagrams for the science classroom with PosterMyWall (www.postermywall.com) or Pixteller (www.pixteller.com).

Share The Why

Teachers may grimace when asked, "Why do we need to know this?", but the question is both appropriate and potentially useful as a catalyst for motivating learners. Students not only need to know what they are expected to learn, but also why they are being asked to learn it. Learners who don't know the intention of a lesson often unnecessarily expend time and energy trying to figure out what their teachers expect them to learn. Some—in their confusion and frustration—give up. For this reason, it is important that students understand what they will be able to know and do when they finish a unit or lesson.

To engage students in your lessons and units, always reinforce the "takeaways" (e.g., "Today, you will learn how to choose an appropriate tool for use in scientific investigation") and the "whys" (e.g., "We are all scientists"; "We all need to understand the world around us"). This practice will motivate students, help you plan effectively, and keep lessons focused on the most critical elements.

Specify Strengths

Give students as much information as you can about their abilities. Talk specifically about what they do well. For example:

> "Your characters are so unique" is more useful than "You are a strong creative writer".

> "You seem to really love solving complex problems" is more useful than "You are a great math student".

> "You are an intuitive actor" is more useful than "You are doing a great job in the play".

> "You are an effective group facilitator" is more useful than "You are a good leader".

> "You handled that conflict with Jay with a lot of maturity" is more useful than "Good job working it out with Jay".

Get It Off The Page

Whenever you start to assign a workbook page, sheet, or problems from the textbook, consider whether or not the content could be taken "off the page." That is, think about whether the material could be taught in a more dynamic way:

› Could you tear up a math worksheet, place the problems around the room, and have students travel to each one and solve it using a clipboard, tablet, or dry erase board?

› Could you take your students outside to run a quarter of a mile, a half of a mile, or a mile as a way to teach those measurements?

› Could those grammar exercises be completed flashcard-style with student partners quizzing one another on the material?

› Could students build a physical model of the rock cycle instead of draw a diagram of it?

› Could you assign book talks instead of book reports?

› Could you tape parts of a timeline on the floor of the classroom and have students walk through an era in history, a series of steps, or a story?

Watch Them Learn

Classroom observation is an assessment appropriate for all ages and all subject areas. It can be a helpful supplement to more formal methods of evaluation, and can give us information that other assessment tools cannot. A formal test cannot tell us, for instance, whether a student is beginning to demonstrate more sophisticated social skills, or whether he or she is becoming a more confident problem solver.

To begin using observation as an assessment, review your standards to see which ones lend themselves to this sort of tool. Establish performance criteria so your observation can be focused. For example, if "holding several stretch positions" is a learning objective, think about what "holding a position" means to you (e.g., How long does the student need to hold the position?).

Then, engage in your observations. Remember to take notes on what matters most and find a method that works well for you. If you live on your tablet, use it to record your observations. If you like to physically add, change, and rearrange your "thoughts" as you work, use colorful sticky notes that you can affix to a binder or notebook at a later time.

Lecture To All

There are many ways to make lecture content more available to your students. Hand out an outline or template to those who may need it ahead of time. Audio or video record certain lessons for students to access more than once. Use plenty of visual supports. Chunk material into smaller segments. Add video clips, relevant music, or short demonstrations for variety. Ask the group to occasionally respond to questions using clickers or dry erase boards. Provide time to discuss big ideas throughout the presentation. Allow students to access fidget items like stress balls or finger puzzles.

Teaching Strategies

Modify Quantity

There are many ways to adapt work. Modifying quantity is one of the easiest ways to personalize an assignment or task. If all students are responsible for reading 25 books a year, a student with an intellectual disability may be required to read 18 books instead. Most students in a kindergarten classroom may be responsible for learning 50 new words in a year, but one student with significant learning differences may be responsible for only half that number. This recommendation can also work to support learners needing enrichment support. Some students may have already mastered the math material and may, therefore, be assigned to complete only the most challenging items on the homework assignment, freeing them to then construct a few of their own problems or explore a related app or website.

Help With Homework

Homework should be just as universally designed as in-class work. One way to follow this guideline is to always assign work that students can do independently. Homework should be skill practice, a chance to extend a lesson that began in class, or an opportunity to explore an upcoming topic. Ideally, completing it should not require additional teaching or adult support.

Another way to adapt homework is to craft it around a student-set goal. One student might work on a goal of learning all her math facts ahead of schedule. Another might want to tackle a challenging novel. Still another may want to choose a handful of activities from the science book and try them at home. Individual plans could be submitted each week, month, or quarter and updated as needed.

Still another way to meet learner needs is to assign the same type of work repeatedly (e.g., read a chapter, write a journal page, watch an instructional video). For a set period of time, the assignment is the same every night. This helps students manage the requirement and gives them opportunities for repeated practice in those tasks selected.

Finally, you may have some learners who need support beyond what is being offered to the class. For these individuals, you may need to eliminate some homework steps or problems, assign minutes instead of tasks to complete (e.g., "Work on your packet for 20 minutes"), or decide to give points not just for correct answers, but also for getting homework in on time and following directions.

Lesson Design

State Your Objective

Students cannot hit a target they do not know about and have not seen. Therefore, it is critical to let learners know exactly what you want them to know and be able to do. Break this down for them so they understand what they will be expected to learn each year, each semester, each unit, and even for each lesson. Some students will need these objectives to be in writing and posted in a prominent spot in the classroom. Others may need a verbal review of the standards and perhaps even a quick decoding of their meaning. For standards that are particularly challenging to understand, consider having students discuss them with a partner before you explain them in a whole-group setting.

Another way to make standards more comprehensible is to break them down into "I can" statements. So, instead of letting students know that the learning objective is "Students will respond to and critique a variety of creations and performances using the artistic foundations," you might present these statements as alternatives: "I can prepare my artwork for public viewing" and "I can revise my work (e.g., project, artwork, presentation) based on others' feedback or self-reflection."

Go Back To The Data

If you're struggling with implementing UDL, examine your assessments, including work samples, in-class formative assessments, standardized tests, and student observations. Look for strengths and opportunities for growth. Explore records and profiles of individual students and of your group or groups as a whole.

Then, use your findings to create the best possible learning experiences.

Use this data to

> create flexible groupings (e.g., reading partners, peer tutor pairings, study groups);

> plan mini-lessons for one, some, or all learners;

> add or change learning materials (e.g., add higher-level reading selections to your classroom library);

> add or change personal supports (e.g., provide more or fewer cues for a student with disabilities);

> explore new collaborative possibilities (e.g., co-plan with the literacy coach to help some students with comprehension); and

> change the nature of instruction for certain lessons (e.g., give students options to work with the group or to self-pace using a textbook or web-based program).

Serve & Learn

Would your students be interested in planting a garden, writing books for younger children, or making quilts for those affected by natural disasters? If so, it might be time to launch service learning projects in your UDL classroom.

Service-learning projects and activities can help teachers individualize instruction and provide challenges to all. Service learning is a particularly valuable tool in a diverse classroom because it allows students to participate in projects with tangible outcomes, make real decisions, speak and be heard, make a difference in the lives of others, and achieve recognition for their accomplishments (Gent, 2009).

This lesson format blends meaningful and thoughtfully planned service or volunteer work with educational goals and critical thinking. For example, having students pick up trash around the school is not service learning; it is a good deed. To elevate this lesson on pollution to service learning, students have to actually explore the problem, generate solutions, and reflect on the process. So, instead of just picking up trash, students might interview local residents about the litter problem, draft plans to keep the area free of waste, clean up the school and surrounding area, reflect on their project, and discuss how grassroots work can affect a community.

See the National Service Learning Clearinghouse for more project ideas: www.servicelearning.org.

Day **354**

Pick At Random

A wide range of groupings should be used throughout the year. Group arrangements should change so that students have opportunities to work with all of their classmates. Sometimes those groupings will be carefully crafted, but other times, you will simply want students to connect with peers that are not necessarily their best pals. In these instances, you will want strategies for randomly grouping the class.

Choose an idea from this list, or design your own idea for making new pairings and groupings:

> Put all student names on craft sticks and pick two or three at a time to form groups.

> Use a deck of cards and have students partner with those with the same/different suit, with those with the same number, etc.

> Buy some inexpensive rubber bracelets and have students find matches or a group representing three, four, or five different colors.

> Use pieces from a boxed memory game and have students find their matching images.

> Purchase two or three each of small gumball machine toys (e.g., plastic animals) and have students find others with the same toy.

> Pass out stickers, have students affix them to their clothing, and direct them to find others with the same image or word.

> Take or collect photos related to an area of content (e.g., pictures of inventors, images of Spanish-speaking nations) and make two or three copies of each so students can form pairs or trios.

> Choose a category (e.g., shoe size, favorite color, number of siblings) and ask students to find someone who is either in the same category or in a different category.

Encourage Writers & Writing

Every teacher is a writing teacher, so look for opportunities to provide writing practice in lessons throughout the day, across subject areas, and using different formats and strategies.

You can, for instance, have students

> write in journals,

> write in interactive notebooks,

> make lists,

> annotate a text,

> post online book reviews,

> blog about learning experiences,

> live Tweet a classroom discussion or presentation,

> pass notes containing content-related questions and comments,

> engage in quick writes and responses during lectures and whole-class discussions,

> write exit card mini-essays,

> try speech recognition software to create short stories,

> create "found poems" with news clippings or magazine articles,

> write sentences or thoughts with magnetic poetry kits, and

> compose letters and notes to authentic audiences (e.g., suggestions to the school board, fan mail to sports figures).

Give It Some Give

Need your classroom to s-t-r-e-t-c-h a bit to meet the needs of all your students? Try using structures with a bit more give. Kelly Chandler-Olcott (2003) has written about what she calls "elastic" instructional frameworks: models and methods of instruction that stretch to accommodate diverse learning needs without requiring students to be labeled or segregated from each other. Such frameworks allow students who are very facile or experienced with a competency or content area to develop skills at increasingly higher levels while simultaneously allowing students who lack certain skills or experiences to acquire them at their own pace.

Without a range of such structures in their repertoire, teachers often end up teaching to the perceived "middle" of their classes, thereby failing to support or to challenge a large number of students who don't fit that profile. Structures that don't stretch much—whole-class oral reading of a single text, for example—have the potential to be disastrous for students with disabilities because many present skills that would be located on the extreme outskirts of a developmental continuum. For this reason, rigid, one-size-fits-all structures are likely to frustrate or bore students with unique learning profiles and they often do not work well for students without disabilities either. Structures that do seem to fit well for a wide range of learners include

> guided reading,

> Daily 5,

> centers or stations,

> computer-based instruction/WebQuests,

> project-based instruction,

> inquiry-based learning,

> drama,

> simulations,

> "flipped" lessons,

> labs,

> service learning, and

> writers' workshops.

Cube It

Cubing is a versatile, easy-to-use instructional strategy that adds a bit of interesting unpredictability to your lessons. To cube a lesson, put students in small groups and give each group a six-sided die with a different direction, question, or prompt on each of its sides. Then, have each student roll the cube and respond to the roll in some way.

If students are analyzing a story, each side of the cube might have a question that will help them retell it or outline pieces of it (e.g., who, what, where, why, when, how). If they are studying a concept or event in social studies such as free elections or westward expansion, the cube might feature options asking them to demonstrate their understanding in some way (e.g., describe, compare, associate, relate, argue for/against, apply).

Cubing can be designed to reach all learners in two different ways. The strategy can be used with different groups using different cubes and, therefore, receiving different prompts. Or you can assign each student in each group a specific side of the cube that best fits their needs or strengths.

Day 358

UDL with MI

It is likely that every educator reading this book is familiar with Howard Gardner's Theory of Multiple Intelligences (MI). Teachers who plan with this theory in mind use a variety of questions such as these:

> How can I use the spoken or written word?

> How can I bring in numbers, logic, or critical thinking?

> How can I use visual aids, visualization, color, art, or metaphor?

> How can I bring in music, or set key points in a rhythm or melody?

> How can I involve the whole body, or hands-on experiences?

> How can I engage students in peer sharing or cooperative learning?

> How can I evoke feelings or memories, or give choices?

> How can I connect this to nature, to classifying, or to observation?

Despite the fact that most teachers are familiar with MI Theory, only some use it as a tool for universally designing lessons, or for making the classroom more accessible. This is unfortunate, as the MI framework can help educators reach many students more effectively. A student who is very social and talkative will benefit from lessons that honor his or her verbal-linguistic intelligence, for instance. In the case of students with disabilities, however, the implications of planning with MI in mind can be even more powerful. Some of these learners will not only be more satisfied with an MI-planned lesson but will also emerge as competent in ways they simply could not in a more traditional lesson. If the teacher allows learners to practice spelling words by tracing them on a friend's back, by including them in a story, by creating rhymes, and by categorizing them by word roots, some will succeed in all or most of these exercises, but others may only be able to remember their words if singing or rhyme are used.

Take Your Stations

Station teaching involves setting up spots in the classroom where small groups of students work on different tasks simultaneously. Stations can involve a wide range of activities including web searches, small-group discussions, independent or partner reading, art or drama exercises, teacher-led mini-lessons, games, brainstorming, video-clip viewings, and examinations of artifacts.

For example, students in a math class might rotate through five stations with specific goals and outcomes such as

> working with the teacher to learn about improper fractions,

> solving fractions problems from the textbook,

> generating real-world applications for using fractions,

> working on fact practice using a choice of two different apps, and

> exploring children's literature about fractions.

One of the satisfying aspects of station teaching is how very easy it is to support the needs of all learners. For instance, any number of adults can be brought into the classroom to facilitate or lead the stations, and many different types of materials can be incorporated into these lessons. Other ideas for creating a UDL lesson with stations include

> offering choices of stations or offering choices within stations;

> labeling one area of the classroom as an enrichment, new tech exploration, or independent project station and letting all students who finish their work visit this station; and

> asking students for ideas on how to make the stations lessons more relevant, challenging, or appealing.

Drop Anchor

In most UDL classrooms, teachers are constantly looking for ways to buy some time with small groups or individual students. One of the easiest ways to do this is to implement an anchor activity.

Anchor activities are tasks that students can work on independently or at least without teacher support. These activities may be assigned when students walk into the classroom, or they can be implemented for some period during a class to give teachers time to engage in individual assessments, or meet with small groups. In essence, anchor activities free teachers from their work at the helm of the classroom, allowing them to designate class time for more personalized interactions with learners.

True anchor activities should always be meaningful and allow students to deepen their understanding of learning standards. They should also allow each learner to work at a different pace and on different content (if necessary or desired), which is why they are so helpful in the UDL classroom. The only requirements of anchor activities are that they must be (a) worthy of a student's time, (b) appropriate to his or her abilities, and (c) easy to enter and exit so that transitions are short.

Examples of anchor activities include

› silent or partner reading;

› independent or partner writing;

› skill practice with peers or with the use of apps/websites;

› project-based instruction with students working alone, with partners, or in small groups; and

› whole-class peer tutoring (e.g., review material).

361

Listen To Russia

Promote content integration. Introduce Russian pop music as students learn about that nation. Teach about probability during science experiments. Count by fives during physical education exercises. Teach annotation during a social studies lesson. Read about current events relevant to your topics of study in health class. Share a content-related picture book during a Spanish lesson. Explore Van Gogh's *Starry Night* as an introduction to the study of the galaxy.

Day 362

Make It Matter

Students connect to information, activities, and experiences that they find relevant, interesting, and personally valuable. In order to hook students and engage them in lessons, consider all of the ways you might make learning matter to them.

Start by offering a wide variety of classroom activities, materials, and experiences. Look to your students for input as you choose these activities, materials, and experiences. Consider their stories, backgrounds, and interests.

In addition, keep your teaching fresh and sprinkled with some suspense, fun, and novelty. Develop a lesson involving students' families. Hint about a new unit before you reveal what it is. Connect learning to pop culture.

Finally, use the following questions to guide your planning:

› Are my lessons age-appropriate?

› Do I plan lessons that are culturally relevant to some or all of my students?

› Do I plan lessons that are socially relevant to some or all of my students?

› Do I plan lessons that are compelling for different racial, ethnic, and gender groups?

If you need resources for planning lessons that matter to all students, browse lesson ideas from Teaching Tolerance (www.tolerance.org) and Pop Culture Classroom (www.popcultureclassroom.org). In addition, check out *The New York Times* article on using current events in the classroom (www.learning.blogs.nytimes.com/2014/10/07/50-ways-to-teach-current-events).

Day 363

Tier It

A tiered lesson is a strategy for meeting the needs of learners in a multi-level classroom. Tiering allows students to take several different paths to meet lesson objectives.

For example, in one area of a primary classroom, students might be using manipulatives (e.g., cotton balls, counting bears) to illustrate single-digit story problems. Another group of students might be engaged in the same task, but be assigned more challenging problems. A third group could work collaboratively to write, illustrate, and solve their own double-digit story problems.

In the example above, the lesson is tiered according to student readiness, but there are many other ways to tier a lesson. You can form groups based on learning profiles or interests, for example.

No matter how you design your tiered lesson, keep in mind that you are not necessarily looking to form groups of equal size. Tiering should give you the freedom to provide the learning experience that is "just right" for any learner. Therefore, in a single lesson, Tier I may have one group of five students, Tier II may include three groups of four students, and Tier III may consist of only one group of two students.

As you try tiering and refine your practice, keep in mind that you will want to regroup students over the course of the year and, perhaps, even over the course of the unit. The idea of flexible groups in this strategy is essential.

Day 364

Light A Spark

Start your units with a spark. Your goal should be to get students engaged and excited about the material.

You might:

› Show a compelling movie clip (e.g., *Gorillas in the Mist* to teach conservation).

› Start with a question (e.g., "What are the differences between _____ and _____?").

› Share a photo essay and have students discuss the images (e.g., microscopic images of cells to kick off a biology unit).

› Perform a short skit (e.g., become Chavez and lead a strike).

› Bring in interesting artifacts (e.g., sugar skulls to study Day of the Dead).

› Play music (e.g., ragtime tunes before studying the early 1900s).

› Launch an open-ended activity involving brainstorming, prediction, or small-group discussion (e.g., "How much sugar do most people consume in a day?" to start a lesson on nutrition).

› Engage in a dramatic reading—possibly with props (e.g., newspaper articles about the moon landing).

Be sure to clearly connect your energizer to the work you will be doing in the unit. Get them anxious to learn more. You might even consider revisiting your energizer at the end of the unit. If you start with one movie clip that asks a question or presents a problem, you might end the unit by showing a clip that answers or resolves it.

Change The Learning State

No matter how compelling our content or dynamic our lecture style, students can only learn effectively in a whole-class format for so long. Current research on the brain and learning suggests that students need to move, talk, and interact regularly in order to learn effectively (Freeman, Eddy, McDonough, Smith, Okoroafor, Jordt & Wenderoth, 2014; Ratey & Hagerman, 2008; Willis, 2007). For older students, shoot for a change every 20 minutes. For younger students, you may need to shift gears after about 10 or 15 minutes.

This recommendation can sound challenging, but changing the learning state does not need to involve major alterations to the lesson. For instance, you might

> engage in a demonstration,

> show a short movie clip,

> play a game,

> lead a brain break,

> lead students in a chant related to content,

> change the learning environment (e.g., dim the lights),

> have students move to another space in the classroom,

> have students stand to act something out,

> play some music,

> ask students to journal and/or draw, or

> ask students to work with a partner or small group.

References

Ainsworth, S., Prain, V. & Tytler, R. (2011).
Drawing to learn in science.
Science, 333(6046), 1096–1097.

Allington, R. (2011).
What really matters for struggling readers.
New York: Pearson.

Anderson, L. W., Krathwohl, D. R., Airasian, P. W.,
Cruikshank, K. A., Mayer, R. E., Pintrich, P. R., Raths, J.,
Wittrock, M. C. (2001).
*A taxonomy for learning, teaching, and assessing: A revision of
Bloom's taxonomy of educational objectives.*
New York: Pearson, Allyn & Bacon.

Andrade, J. (2010).
What does doodling do?
Applied Cognitive Psychology, 24, 100–106.

Barnes, M. & Gonzalez, J. (2015).
Hacking education.
Cleveland, OH: Times 10 Publications.

Buehl, D. (2001).
Classroom strategies for interactive learning (2nd ed.).
Newark, DE: The International Reading Association.

Chandler-Olcott, K. (2003).
Seeing all students as literate.
In P. Kluth, D. Straut, & D. Biklen (Eds.).
*Access to academics for all students: critical approaches to inclusive
curriculum, instruction, and policy* (pp. 69–84).
Mahwah, NJ: Lawrence Erlbaum Associates.

Dodge, B. (1995).
Webquests: A technique for internet-based learning.
Distance Educator 1(2), 10-13.

Dweck, C. S. (2006).
Mindset: The new psychology of success.
New York: Random House.

Freeman, S., Eddy, S. L., McDonough, M., Smith, M. K., Okoroafor, N., Jordt, H., & Wenderoth, M. P. (2014). Active learning increases student performance in science, engineering, and mathematics.
Proceedings of the National Academy of Sciences, 111(23), 8410–8415.

Gent, P. J. (2009).
Great ideas: Using service-learning and differentiated instruction to help your students succeed.
Baltimore, MD: Paul H. Brookes.

Goldberg, M. (1993).
A portrait of Ted Sizer.
Educational Leadership, 51(1), 53-56.

Kagan, S. (1989).
The structural approach to cooperative learning.
Educational Leadership, 47(4), 12–15.

Kagan, S. (1994).
Cooperative learning.
San Clemente, CA: Kagan Publishing.

Kluth, P. & Chandler-Olcott, K. (2007).
A land we can share: Teaching literacy to students with autism.
Baltimore: Paul H. Brookes.

Kluth, P. & Danaher, S. (2013).
From text maps to memory caps.
Baltimore: Paul H. Brookes.

Ladson-Billings, G. (1994).
The dreamkeepers: Successful teachers of African-American students.
San Francisco, CA: Jossey-Bass.

Meyer, A., Rose, D. H. & Gordon, D. (2014).
Universal design for learning: Theory and practice.
Wakefield, MA: CAST Professional Publishing.

O'Donnell-Allen (2006).
The book club companion: Fostering strategic readers in the secondary classroom.
Portsmouth, NH: Heinemann.

Pink, D. (2011).
Drive: The surprising truth about what motivates us.
New York: Canongate.

Ratey, J. & Hagerman, E. (2008).
Spark: The revolutionary new science of exercise and the brain.
New York: Little, Brown and Company.

Rose, D. H. (2001).
Universal design for learning: Deriving guiding principles from networks that learn.
Journal of Special Education Technology 16(1), 66-70.

Rose, D. H. & Meyer, A. (2002).
Teaching every student in the digital age: Universal design for learning.
Alexandria, VA: ASCD.

Wiggins, G. (2012).
7 keys to effective feedback.
Educational Leadership, 70(1), 11–16.

Willis, J. (2007).
Brain-friendly strategies for the inclusion classroom.
Alexandria, VA: Association for Supervision and Curriculum Development.

Zike, D. (1992).
Big book of books.
San Antonio: Dinah-Might Adventures.

Literary References

Bao Lord, B. (1984).
In the year of the boar and Jackie Robinson.
New York: HarperCollins.

Cisneros, S. (1989).
The house on Mango Street.
New York, NY: Random House.

Danticat, E. (2010).
Eight days: A story of Haiti.
New York: Orchard Books.

George, J. (1972).
Julie of the wolves.
New York: HarperCollins.

Griffey, H. (1998).
Earthquakes and other natural disasters.
New York: DK Publishing.

Gwynne, F. (1970).
The king who rained.
New York: Simon & Schuster.

Janeczko, P. (2009).
A kick in the head.
Somerville, MA: Candlewick.

Lee, H. (1960).
To kill a mockingbird.
New York: Warner Books.

McKissack, P. (1992).
A million fish . . . more or less.
New York. Alfred A. Knopf.

Polacco, P. (1994).
Pink and Say.
New York: Philomel Books.

Rubin, A. (2008).
Those darn squirrels.
New York: Houghton Mifflin Harcourt.

Simon, S. (2006).
Earthquakes.
New York: HarperCollins.

Using This Book

You likely have your own ideas for using *Universal Design Daily*, but I wanted to share a few of my own before you put this book down. Peruse these suggestions and choose one or more to get started.

Educators

> Use *Universal Design Daily* as the title suggests and explore a single idea each day.

> Form a book club and meet after reading each of the three sections.

> Work as a team to study the book; have everyone in your grade level or department try a handful of ideas each month and provide feedback on the implementation of them.

> Open the book to a random page each week and read what you see; use the idea in an upcoming plan.

> Share the book with your students in upper grades. Ask them to choose an idea or two they would like to try (as classroom co-teachers) or have you try.

> Keep the book out as you plan; page through it to find inspiration.

Administrators

› Share one idea each day in an e-mail blast or on an internal website.

› Have a team of teachers work together to try all 365 ideas in one year. Have them document their progress and share their findings with colleagues.

› Ask teams to test ideas in the book for a few weeks and blog about their experience.

› Tear the pages out of the book and wallpaper your faculty lounge with ideas...literally!

› Challenge your staff to try every single idea in the book. Check off the ideas as they are attempted and/or integrated and provide feedback on their progress.

› Model one UDL idea from this book in each one of your faculty meetings. Use a variety of visuals, integrate a group activity, or incorporate a new tech tool as you present or discuss an issue.

› Ask teachers in your school or district to try different ideas and to post short videos or photographs of their efforts on an internal wiki.

Therapists, Counselors & Social Workers

› Look through the book for ideas that can be used as you collaborate with teachers. Would any of the tech tools recommended help your students with writing tasks? Are there learning materials you might want to try or suggest to your colleagues? Are there professional development opportunities you would want to try?

› Identify a handful of suggestions that you can use to co-plan or co-teach with general and special education teachers. For example, a physical therapist might have several ideas for integrating student IEP goals into the idea featured on *Day 296*, which is taking a content-based walk around the school and neighborhood.

› Choose one idea from each UDL-related section (Methods of Engagement, Methods of Action and Expression, and Methods of Representation) and implement it with a colleague as a way to become more acquainted with the language and practices of universal design.

Paraprofessionals

› Look through this book with your team and identify strategies that might work well for students you support. Are there new ways you might work in the classroom? Can you identify new and potentially useful visual supports, teaching strategies, or apps for one, some, or more learners with identified needs?

› Read through the three sections specifically focused on universal design to learn more about this model of planning.

› Look specifically at the section on collaboration and identify one or more ways to work with colleagues to better support students. You might take the advice on *Day 224* and "think beyond 1:1", for instance.

Families

› Peruse the book with your PTO and highlight ways you might help educators reach their UDL-related goals (e.g., sponsor professional development related to UDL).

› Read the book and highlight ideas that might work well for your child. This suggestion may be especially useful for families of students with disabilities or unique learning profiles.

› Page through these ideas and consider how you might partner with your child's teacher or teachers. Could you donate supplies for universally-designed lessons (see *Day 14: Stock Up*); help to develop classroom tools (see *Day 24: Create a Coffee Klatch*); or offer to support UDL-related goals (see *Day 205: Volunteer for Volunteers*)?

About the Author

Dr. Paula Kluth is a consultant, author, advocate, and independent scholar who works with teachers and families to provide inclusive opportunities for students with disabilities and to create more responsive and engaging schooling experiences for all learners. Paula is a former special educator and inclusion facilitator who has worked in both high schools and elementary schools. She has also served as a university professor, teaching courses on implementing inclusive education and supporting diverse learners.

Most recently, Paula's work has centered on helping teachers and administrators educate all students in their schools and classrooms. She also frequently works with families and advocacy groups to support goals related to inclusive education and schools for all.

Paula has won several awards in her field. She is the recipient of The PEAL [Parent Education & Advocacy Leadership] Center's Inclusive Education Champion Award; The National Down Syndrome Congress's Educator of the Year; and The Belle Center of Chicago's Inclusion Advocate of the Year.

Paula is the author or co-author of more than 15 books and products including:

From Tutor Scripts to Talking Sticks: 100 Ways to Differentiate Instruction in K-12 Inclusive Classrooms (with Sheila Danaher);

From Text Maps to Memory Caps: 100 More Ways to Differentiate Instruction in K-12 Inclusive Classrooms (with Sheila Danaher);

30 Days to the Co-Taught Classroom: How to Create an Amazing, Nearly Miraculous & Frankly Earth-Shattering Partnership in One Month or Less (with Julie Causton);

"Don't We Already Do Inclusion?": 100 Ways to Improve Inclusive Schools;

"You're Going to Love This Kid": Teaching Students with Autism in Inclusive Classrooms;

Joyful Learning: Active and Collaborative Learning in the Inclusive Classroom (with Alice Udvari-Solner);

A Land We Can Share: Teaching Literacy to Students with Autism (with Kelly Chandler-Olcott);

You're Welcome: 30 Innovative Ideas for the Inclusive Classroom (with Patrick Schwarz);

"Just Give Him the Whale": 20 Ways to Use Fascinations, Areas of Expertise, and Strengths to Support Students with Autism (with Patrick Schwarz); and

The Autism Checklist: A Practical Reference for Parents and Teachers (with John Shouse).

Go Online!

Learn more about Paula on her webpage: www.paulakluth.com

Get Social!

You can also connect on social media including on Facebook, Twitter, and Pinterest:

 Facebook
www.facebook.com/paulakluth

 Twitter
twitter.com/PaulaKluth

 Pinterest
www.pinterest.com/paulapin

50407507R00232

Made in the USA
San Bernardino, CA
22 June 2017